TRANSFIGURATION

30 Meditations Inspired by Transforming Trauma & Spirituality

TRANSFIGURATION

*30 Meditations Inspired by Transforming
Trauma & Spirituality*

AVA DASYA RASA

de Profundis Press
Albuquerque, NM

TRANSFIGURATION, 30 Meditations Inspired by Transforming Trauma & Spirituality.

Copyright 2023 © Ava Dasya Rasa

All rights reserved. No portion of this book may be reproduced, stored in a retrieval system, or transmitted in any form or by any means—electronic, mechanical, photocopy, recording, scanning, or other—except for brief quotations in critical reviews or articles, without the prior written permission of the author and publisher.

This book is not intended to be a substitute for the advice, counsel, or medical recommendations by medical, psychological, or mental health professionals. Nor is it intended to be a substitute for Spiritual Direction. Rather, it is intended to offer information and inspiration to help the reader collaborate with their health care providers and Spiritual Directors as they seek optimal well-being. We advise the reader to consider carefully the ideas presented in this book and to seek advice from qualified professionals before attempting to use them.

The Bible passages used in this book are from the World English Bible, with Deuterocanon Apocrypha, 2020 (WEB), which is in the public domain.

Quotes at the start of each theme that are in the public domain have appropriate attributions.

Every effort has been made to ensure that all the information in this book is accurate at the time of publication; however, de Profundis Press neither endorses nor guarantees the content of external links referenced in this book.

Published 2023
Published by de Profundis Press
Contact: deprofundispress@gmail.com
Graphic Designer: Shrikesh Kumar
Cover Photo by Annie Spratt on Unsplash
Printed in the United States of America
First Edition

ISBN: 979-8-9874042-0-1 (Paperback)
ISBN: 979-8-9874042-3-2 (Hard cover)
ISBN: 979-8-9874042-6-3 (eBook)

Library of Congress Control Number: 2022922580

Print and bound in the United States of America

To my clients, who have entrusted me with the gift of companioning them through their transformational healing of transfiguration,

Deep Bows

PREFACE

TRANSFIGURATION, 30 Meditations Inspired by Transforming Trauma and Spirituality, has its genesis in both my personal experience as a trauma survivor, who underwent a radical process of transforming trauma, and my collaboration with and bearing witness to psychotherapy clients who have gifted me with the privilege of companioning them on their transformational healing journeys. I am a Licensed Clinical Social Worker, LCSW-C, having earned a Master's in Social Work (MSW), as well as a Master of Arts in Theology (MA); and I earned a graduate Certificate in Religion, Gender, and Sexuality from Vanderbilt Divinity School. My theological studies were centered in both social ethics and mysticism. I am grounded in a contemplative spirituality practice of Centering Prayer spanning more than four decades.

I am a transpersonal psychotherapist specializing in trauma, grief, and contemplative spirituality & renewal. My clinical training is rooted in the neurobiology of trauma, somatic and relational neuroscience, polyvagal theory, and attachment research, including trauma attachment. I specialize in Neuro-based, Somatic Trauma Therapies, such as: Brainspotting, EMDR, Somatic-Attachment, and Trauma-Sensitive Mindfulness, which are informed and buttressed by adjunct therapies such as: Depth Psychotherapy, Internal Family Systems (IFS), Grief Recovery, Dialectical Behavior Therapy (DBT), and Contemplative Spirituality & Renewal.

Transforming trauma, an embodied interior transfiguring process, leads to post-traumatic spiritual growth. We are soul-wounded. This soul-wounding is about how we are severed from our authentic selves at the deepest place in us, the numinous terrain of our souls, our embodied being.[1] The embodied interior transformational journey of transfiguration takes us to all the places in ourselves that we have avoided out of fear—fear of punishment, fear of rejection, fear of failure, and fear of success; or, out of self-hatred, toxic shame, separation anxiety, and social stigma. It is about recognizing that our trauma wounds are not solely psychological, emotional, biological, or physical wounds. Rather, they are, at their core, spiritual wounds wrapped up in our biopsychosocial selves. By spiritual I do not mean religious.

Spirituality is the conscious awareness of and connection to the sacred, something both deeply within us and all of creation *and* with something altogether beyond our immediate selves. It is about connection with the immanent and the transcendent. Some people experience spirituality relationally in community; others in the solitude of their "cell," or inner monastery, and others still in nature. Spirituality is about entering into both our human condition fully, touching on something that is immediate and immanent; and it also is about entering into an experience of something that is beyond us that is infinite and transcendent. Our encounters with the sacred pierce the veil of our surface lives, revealing something of the deeply psycho-spiritual embodied divine, or *holy* within.

Transfiguration is a process of metamorphosis by which we transform our trauma that is stored in our body—it is a holistic journey involving our body's biology and sensations, our mind's observations and cognitions, and our unconscious and most authentic selves that are hidden, yet always already rooted in the numinous terrain of our soul, our embodied being. We are souls, embodied beings—and hidden in the numinous terrain of our embodied beingness, are both our authentic selves and the Infinite, the seat of all love and Divine Empathy.[2] This book is about how we can radically transform our trauma, so that we live fully into a transformative healed, transfigured life—our authentic selves, a place of belonging.

Transfiguration is a transformative process that involves coming into intimate contact with all our ruptured, broken and bleeding, lost and confused, fragmented and frightened humanity; and realizing our exquisite capacity for resilience, self-acceptance, lovingkindness, empathy, compassion, receptivity, hospitality, and transformation. Transformational healing, leading to transfiguration, is, I believe, the most important personal responsibility we can engage in during our time on this planet.

Without intimate self-knowledge, which comes only by diving into the deep beneath the surface of our waking lives, without transforming the wounded, fragmented parts of ourselves[3]—the infant, child, teen, and young adult, without meeting our emotional energies where we are most vulnerable and learning how to take ownership of them, express and regulate them, and without accessing our very souls, our embodied being, from which our most authentic selves emerge and from where we can touch the Infinite, we are left alienated, lost, confused, frightened, depressed, angry, anxiety-ridden, emotionally dysregulated, estranged from ourselves, unable to tolerate any distress, sick in body, and spiritually bankrupt. Post-traumatic spiritual growth emerges from the survivor undergoing a radical metamorphosis—a transfiguration.

At all junctures in this transformational journey, we are called to walk through thresholds of returning,[4] sacred gateways or portals, which lead us deeper into our embodied interior landscape. It all begins, though, with a trauma, individual or collective: an illness, relational or sexual violence, military or combat experience, racial oppression and discrimination, poverty, natural disasters, terrorism, gun violence, or religious abuse. Trauma is something that happens both to us and in us. According to Bessel van der Kolk, psychiatrist, neuroscientist, author, and international pioneer and leader in traumatic stress-related studies, trauma is both an overwhelming experience impacting our central nervous systems, and trauma is related to whether or not we have someone there at the time of the trauma to help us cope.[5] Trauma is both an event that is unmanageable and it is the neurobiological impact that is left on our central nervous system leaving us feeling the pain, fear, and other distressing emotions.

My intention in authoring this book is to reassure all trauma survivors they are not alone. They are not crazy. They are not bad. Rather, they are among millions of other survivors of trauma, who have suffered traumatic stress responses to unhealthy, abusive, or devastating situations, relationships, and environments. Whether they have received psychiatric diagnoses, such as: Post-Traumatic Stress Disorder, or PTSD, Complex PTSD, or C-PTSD, Dissociative Disorders, a depressive or anxiety disorder, or borderline personality disorder (BPD), their experiences of betrayal, abandonment, estrangement from self, relational conflicts, self-destructive and self-harming behaviors, re-enactment of traumas, and overall total self-loathing are, in large part, neurobiologically driven responses to trauma.

Transfiguration

These emotional experiences and behaviors are symptoms that are connected to our adaptive responses to toxic, abusive, violent, or other unexpected or unhealthy wounding experiences. They are connected to our animal defenses rooted in the neurobiology of our brain's limbic systems. Transforming trauma will result in our less than optimal coping defense mechanisms morphing into healthy, sound, sane, skillful, self-soothing, and secure responses that will enable us to live beyond surviving to thriving!

I authored this book to affirm that the fruit of transforming trauma is our transfiguration. Transfiguration necessitates us offering our false, maladaptive, performative selves to undergo a radical transformation as we return to our authentic selves. This will necessarily involve learning how to establish safety and stability, as we acknowledge, befriend, and love the ruptured, fragmented, estranged aspects of ourselves. This involves our self-emptying of all that impedes our ability to be our authentic, transfigured selves. To begin this radical healing process, we need to be in a safe container[6] relationship, wherein we are unconditionally accepted and affirmed, and in which we can begin to co-regulate our nervous systems and explore and express ourselves. This book also serves as a poetic and practical resource for therapists and spiritual directors who serve trauma survivors. It can provide insight into companioning others on their transformational journeys, as well as support themselves in their own transformational healing and spiritual paths.

Transfiguration is the journey of plumbing the depths of our embodied interior landscape, traversing the subtle yet complex geography of our hearts and touching the numinous terrain of our souls. Embarking on a transformational, transfiguring journey is an act of courage, humility, and grace. As we transform our lived traumas, layer upon layer, a renewed spirituality emerges, because post-traumatic spiritual growth is not only possible but also inevitable.

Lastly, a word about the title of this book, TRANSFIGURATION. In Christian theology, the Transfiguration story is told in all three synoptic gospels: Matthew 17:1-8, Mark 9:2-8, and Luke 9:28-36. Matthew states, "After six days, Jesus took with him Peter, James, and John his brother, and brought them up into a high mountain by themselves. He was changed before them. His face shone like the sun, and his garments became as white as the light. Behold, Moses and Elijah appeared to them talking with him. Peter answered and said to Jesus, "Lord, it is good for us to be here. If you want, let's make three tents here: one for you, one for Moses, and one for Elijah." While he was still speaking, behold, a bright cloud overshadowed them. Behold, a voice came out of the cloud, saying, "This is my beloved Son, in whom I am well pleased. Listen to him." When the disciples heard it, they fell on their faces, and were very afraid. Jesus came and touched them and said, "Get up, and don't be afraid." Lifting up their eyes, they saw no one,

Transfiguration

except Jesus alone" (Matt. 17: 1-8). This is the traditional Christian biblical story of the Transfiguration.

I use the term transfiguration in this book to point to the radical change that unfolds holistically when we seek to transform our trauma. When we are transfigured, we, too, become illumined in body, mind, spirit, and soul. This means we become conscious, aware, and connected to our thoughts, emotions, and body sensations; we become reconnected to our embodied senses. We come to know ourselves intimately—psycho-emotionally, physically, and spiritually, as we navigate our embodied interior landscape. We become more spiritually attuned with ourselves, others, and the whole of creation. We undergo a transformation on multiple levels of our personhood, and through this transformational process, we become our authentic selves—and we inevitably encounter the Divine Indwelling, the Infinite, or Mystery.

We come to understand we are not separated from the divine, one another, or creation. We emerge from the transformational journey changed from the inside out: we reframe our life experiences with empathy and self-compassion, because through our transformational healing, we internalize healthy attachment relations with our wounded selves; we learn how to regulate our emotions which includes self-soothing, and we are at home in our own bodies, attuning to our implicit felt sense of our experiences. We learn how to sustain social engagement states, where we experience relational connectivity, creativity, curiosity, and an overall openness, or receptivity to life. We learn how to love ourselves unconditionally. As we pass through the thresholds of returning, gateways or portals, that I set forth, we venture into our embodied interior landscape and discover our authentic selves.

This is our return. This is our transfiguration: we are radically changed psycho-emotionally, physically, and spiritually. As we pass through thresholds of returning, we transform. Our soul-wounding becomes the threshold to our soul-mending, or transfiguration. Our thresholds of returning are sacred gateways or portals through which we pass and emerge with a renewed spirituality.

We are changed. We are made anew. With new-found resiliency and a renewed spirituality, we rewrite our trauma tales discovering fresh meaning and purpose. We return to our lives with a revisioning of our life mission. Through our transfiguration, we become who we are meant to be; and, in doing so, we come home to our authentic selves—a place of belonging.

Ava Dasya Rasa
Albuquerque, NM
December, 2022

CONTENTS

Introduction 1
1. Rupture 11
2. Crisis 14
3. Embarking 18
4. Safety 21
5. Crushed in Spirit 26
6. Darkness 31
7. Befriending 36
8. Surrender 40
9. Bread of Affliction 44
10. *Metánoia* 47
11. Lamentations 50
12. Waiting 55
13. *Kenosis* 60
14. Self-Compassion 65
15. Enfleshed 69
16. Solitude 75

17. *Holy* Listening 81
18. Desert Wilderness 84
19. *Kintsugi* 89
20. Presence 92
21. Silence 97
22. Forgiveness.. 102
23. Bearing Witness 107
24. *Hesed*... 112
25. Contemplative Prayer.. 116
26. Oil of Mercy.. 123
27. Transfiguration 126
28. Begin Again 130
29. Authenticity.. 137
30. Awe 140

Epilogue.. 145

Appendix A: Guidelines for Centering Prayer 147

Notes... 149

Bibliography 156

Further Recommended Reading..................................... 164

Acknowledgements.. 167

About the Author 169

INTRODUCTION

TRANSFIGURATION is a compilation of 30 contemplative meditations inspired by transforming trauma and spirituality. These poetic meditations arise out of both my clinical experience as a transpersonal psychotherapist, who specializes in trauma, grief, and contemplative spirituality and renewal; and as one who has transformed my own trauma wounds by walking the contemplative path, while simultaneously undergoing intensive psychotherapy and trauma recovery. While my experience of transforming trauma informs these meditations, this is not an autobiography. I penned the content in this book, including the 30 Meditations, Intentional Invitations, Reverent Reflections, and the quotes at the start of five themes: 14 Self-Compassion, 21 Silence, 23 Bearing Witness, 25 Contemplative Prayer, and 27 Transfiguration.

Trauma

What do I mean by trauma? The origin of the word trauma is Greek, τραύμα, and it means, "wound." It seems that the term "trauma" has now become ubiquitous. This is for good reason—ours is a world wherein each person is impacted by trauma, be it individual or collective. Trauma is common. Collectively, we are wounded by a multitude of traumatic events: the ongoing climate crisis of our magnificent planet—we become disrupted witnessing wildfires consuming massive swaths of our forests and mountains; we weep for and with those victims who are devastated by natural disasters that destroy virtually everything in their path. We are profoundly angered and saddened to realize the pervasive unethical treatment, cruelty, and abuse of our fellow creatures, other species. We fall to our knees with hearts shattered into a thousand pieces each time we learn of yet another tragic incident of gun violence in our schools, churches, synagogues, outdoor venues, and in our homes and streets.

We are devastated by economic losses that leave us crushed, feeling hopeless and worried. We are deeply distressed and threatened by systemic racism and oppression. We are anxious and unable to sleep because of violations of fundamental human rights against diverse and vulnerable peoples, imminent threats of violence and terrorism (domestic and foreign), and the troubling rise of authoritarianism across our globe. We are filled with unexpressed anger, rage, sadness, hurt, and grief as we muddle through our busy days and nights.

Moreover, many of us walk around with unprocessed, unresolved, and unintegrated personal trauma wounding inside of us that we have carried for years, often decades since childhood. We are living increasingly with real life acute traumas and ongoing chronic or complex traumas. Some of us carry live traumas inside us, including physical abuse and emotional neglect, sexual assault, accidents, economic losses, suicides, bullying, domestic violence, medical traumas, and micro-aggressions, especially related to race, ethnicity, sexual orientation, and gender identity.

Whether our traumas are individual or collective, or both, we feel the reality of traumas in our lives. Trauma adversely impacts the survivor in all aspects of our life: personal, familial, social, educational, and occupational, as it also influences a person's whole self—biological, psychological, social, and spiritual. How our central nervous systems responded to feelings of overwhelm determines the physiological and neurological signature left on us with traces of pain, fear, terror, despair, and more. We feel the effects of trauma in our bodies, where all trauma is stored; and we feel the effects of trauma in our hearts, minds, and souls. Trauma overwhelms us. We hurt.

Transforming trauma often comes about because our broken, bleeding lives are no longer working, and we find ourselves lost, frustrated, angry, and confused—and, at a what I like to call a "Kairos moment," or turning point. Kairos, καιρός, is an ancient Greek word meaning "the right or opportune moment." The ancient Greeks had two words for time, Chronos and Kairos. While the former refers to chronological, sequential, or linear time; the latter signifies "a time in between," a moment of undetermined period in which "something new" or special happens—turning points, Kairos moments, or sacred time. In the Bible, Kairos is about quality time, the "now" time, or the divinely appointed time. These in-between moments are our Kairos moments, our now moments, which hold the possibility for radical transformation from the inside out.

Such a Kairos moment comes when we are overwhelmed and unable to get our bearings. When we know we are no longer able to continue our lives as we have been living them. Our foundational safety has been disrupted. Despite attempts to self-medicate our pain with people, places, or things, we continue to suffer and feel helpless in isolation. We relive our traumas in body, mind, spirit, and soul. Trauma changes our brains. Our autonomic nervous systems respond automatically when a threat is perceived, activating our dysregulated states of trauma defenses: fight, flight, freeze, fawn[7] or fold (collapse). We feel threatened, unsafe, terrified, and mobilized; or we feel disconnected, depressed, helpless, and immobilized. We are in survival mode. We still hurt.

Thresholds of Returning

These 30 meditations take us through thresholds of returning, sacred gateways or portals, which lead us into transformational healing, or transfiguration. These different thresholds are intersecting. They invite us to metaphorically walk through them and turn towards the wounded aspects of ourselves, encountering our chaos and confusion. Transfiguration unfolds simultaneously as we transform our wounded, fragmented selves into our authentic selves. These are not successive stages of transformation but a simultaneous transfiguring process.

Transformational healing of trauma is a process by which our false, maladaptive, performative selves that kept us alive and helped us survive, are deeply changed through our encountering both our soul-wounds and our most authentic selves. Healing from trauma necessitates the engagement of our imagination, as we co-create our lives, transforming them from what I call the *bread of affliction* into infinite possibilities for a renewed life of *awe*—our journey out from our suffering into dwelling in the possibility of a different, transformed, transfigured spiritually rooted life.

The transformational healing process is one that cannot and ought not happen quickly. Rather, to transform, to heal deeply, takes time and patience, as we want to attend to various aspects of ourselves that emerge as we venture into our embodied interior life. We want to prevent experiencing flooding, or feeling overwhelmed and dysregulated with intense emotions, somatic memories, and re-traumatization; or, feeling no emotions, numbed out, shut down, or collapsed.

The metamorphosis that we undergo starts in various places for different people; yet, wherever we begin, we must do so within a safe space. Safety[8] is the linchpin for our ability to heal. Without establishing relational and neurobiological safety, we will not be able to move forward in our transformational healing of trauma. Safety allows a trauma survivor to stabilize. According to Judith Lewis Herman, MD, a second core component of our recovery from trauma is remembrance and mourning.[9] Because of the somatization of trauma, our remembering is rooted in our implicit memories and embodiment, rather than strictly a cognitive grasp or intellectual chronological recall of specific memories. This juncture often reveals some of the most difficult and meaningful dimensions of transforming trauma.

Once we can engage and move through our *lamentations*, as I call them, along with various other thresholds of returning, we can begin to explore the meaning and value in our traumatic histories, as we re-regulate our emotional energies. Eventually, we discern new meaning, discover innate gifts, revision our life calling, and elect to bring our transfiguration offerings back to our communities as our authentic selves in service to others.

Soul-Wounding to Soul-Mending, or Transfiguration

Each of the 30 contemplative meditations begins with a theme. Each meditation theme is followed by a quote pointing to something of the spirit of the meditation. Each meditation explores the theme through a contemplative lens, informed by various somatic and neuro-based, trauma-informed clinical insights gleaned from working with trauma survivors. Each meditation is then followed by an "Intentional Invitation," in which I offer the reader opportunities to sit with the content of the meditation, and contemplatively consider questions or engage in creative practices that are meant to be prompts to awaken insights into our experiences of trauma. This invitation is followed by a "Reverent Reflection." This can be a poem, a poetic reflection, or a poem-prayer. I encourage readers to reflect on their own post-traumatic growth and spirituality and to ask themselves: What spiritual meaning-making emerges from my experience?

The outline of these meditations is not meant to imply that our transformational healing journey is linear. It is not. Rather, the various thresholds of returning are points of entry into the inherently circular, infinite transformative nature of our healing—a transfiguring process. This book can be read sequentially, as each theme connects thematically to the next; or any single meditation can be read discretely as a point of contemplative reflection. Transforming trauma is fluid and malleable. It unfolds a bit differently for each person. It happens gradually, over time, optimally within a safe therapeutic relationship and contemplative spirituality practice.

Some people start transformational healing with their experience of "Rupture," while others with their experience of "Darkness;" and others still with "Crushed in Spirit." Wherever we start our transforming of trauma, we start where we find ourselves at any given moment. There is no right or wrong, no one-size fits all. Once we experience a pivotal point that sets us on our path to transformational healing, then we each do need to establish safety before having the ability to move forward.

The journey from soul-wounding to soul-mending, or transfiguration, is not for the faint of heart. There are perils involved, as we must have willingness to explore and examine our own selves with curiosity, which includes challenging some of our assumptions, biases, and predilections. Our desire to be radically transformed will necessarily outweigh any other priority. We must be willing to do the hard work of inner transformational healing. So *will and desire* play a central role in whether we actually embark and travel the path of transformation towards transfiguration.

If we give ourselves over fully, wholeheartedly, openly, and humbly to the transformational healing journey of soul-wounding to soul-mending, or transfiguration, we will inevitably walk through the thresholds of returning that are most necessary for us to arrive at our most authentic self—a place of belonging: fully alive, fully aware, fully present in this moment, and rooted in *hesed,* or the lovingkindness ever unfolding beneath the numinous terrain our soul, our embodied being.

EPIGRAPH

The fish cannot drown in the water,
the bird cannot sink in the air,
gold cannot perish in the fire,
where it gains its clear and shining worth.
God has granted to each creature
to cherish its own nature.
How can I withstand my own nature?

—Mechthild of Magdeburg

1
RUPTURE

"Man by suffering shall learn. So the heart of him, again aching with remembered pain, bleeds and sleepeth not, until wisdom comes against his will."
—Aeschylus

Rupture. To break, burst, crack, tear, fissure, rip, or split. These are seven meanings of rupture. There are more. When we experience rupture, it is as if we are being torn apart at the seams. Ripped from our comfort zones. Split in half. Cracked. We begin to recognize the fissures in our broken lives. Rupture can feel like the world is a life-threatening place—unwelcoming, dangerous, and terrifying. We feel unsafe. We feel betrayed. We might even feel as if we are unable to move or act. We experience a sense of I am here, and I am not here. Not being. Disappearing. Untethered. Or we feel dissociated. Unable to speak. Unable to move. Depressed. Disconnected from our emotions and bodies. We are numb. We shut down. We do nothing.

Traumatic rupture can also feel like there is too much chaos in the world. Our life is unmanageable. We feel overwhelmed and out of control. We have trouble with concentration, memory loss, interpersonal relations, and hopelessness. We feel hypervigilant, or highly energized with rushes of energy and flashbacks. In this state we misread social and facial cues as angry or aggressive. We are irritable. On edge. We rage. We blame. We are impulsive. We may engage in suicidality and self-harm, such as cutting ourself. We may engage in addictions and eating disorder behaviors. We may experience insomnia, a loss of interest, isolation. We are edgy, alert, angry, panicked, and overwhelmed. We experience our nervous systems being chronically overactivated, hijacked, dysregulated. We do not possess the capacity to stay within our window of tolerance.[10]

We are filled with shame and blame and self-loathing. We feel utterly overwhelmed. We might extend ourselves to others, going out of our way to please everyone else at our own expense, so as to avoid "rocking the boat," or fawning, pleasing and appeasing,[11] just to survive; we attempt to accommodate another's needs, usually a perpetrator or one that is threatening our safety, so as to neutralize any potential of abuse or injury. Or we feel as if we will collapse. Faint. Feign death. Become entirely immobilized. Something is awry. Up until now, we have been able to fool everyone, performing on the outside as if nothing is wrong. Absolutely nothing. In fact, we may be overachievers on the outside. Perfectionists. Accomplished. On the inside, however, we are suffering.

We know something is off. We feel disrupted by our emotions, thoughts, and bodily responses. We might want to abandon ourselves.

When a person who has historical trauma, including developmental, acute, chronic, or complex trauma, realizes that nothing is working anymore, that they have lost their way, that everything they thought was intact is now in tatters, then they begin to enter a threshold of returning through their embodied, lived experience of traumatic rupture, or soul-wounding. Another way of conceptualizing this rupture is to think of it as a *crisis*, or an initiation hurling us into transforming our trauma.

~

Intentional Invitation

Choose a creative expression—journal writing, painting, drawing, clay work, or composing music to express your insights into the following two questions: 1. What is my understanding of my rupture? 2. What is my greatest fear in this rupture?

Reverent Reflection

> I am lonely—
> a black bird
> perched on
> a roof
> sounding
> an alarm
> call

2
CRISIS

"Your pain is the breaking of the shell that encloses your understanding."
—Khalil Gibran

When we experience a traumatic rupture, we are in an autonomic nervous system survival response, or what feels like a *crisis* experience neuro-biologically, psycho-emotionally, and somatically. According to Stephen W. Porges, PhD, we have three neural circuits: 1. social engagement, or the ventral vagal state; 2. The sympathetic nervous system; and 3. the dorsal vagal state.[12] These three states have attending threat responses that include: fight, flight, and freeze—a chronic freeze response is also known as "tonic immobility,"[13] fawn and fold (collapse). Some of us will experience hyper-arousal with our sympathetic nervous system mobilizing us into either fight or flight. Our lens becomes myopic, narrowing our ability to ascertain the full spectrum of what is happening. We might want to move towards a perceived threat and fight or move away in flight, fleeing for our safety. Or we may experience a freeze response, a hyperarousal state and a trauma response that is stimulated by the dorsal branch of the vagal nerve,[14] a parasympathetic nervous system activation, where we are frozen, unable to move or act. We are immobilized.

Others experience a fawn response, stimulated by our ventral vagal nerve and our dorsal vagal nerve,[15] where we engage in pleasing and appeasing others so as to avoid abuse, neglect, chaos, and conflict. Some of us may experience what is known as attach-cry[16], which, like the freeze and fawn responses, is a crossover response, involving both the ventral vagal and dorsal vagal states. Or some of us might become so immobilized by the trauma threat that we experience hypo-arousal to the point of fold, or collapse, which is stimulated by our dorsal vagal nerve in the parasympathetic nervous system.[17] This is where some of us will experience dissociation and no social engagement. We feel so overwrought with the perceived threat, we either focus on pleasing others so as to avoid criticism, conflict, or injury; or we numb out, shut down, and collapse.

If we are living with Complex Post-Traumatic Stress Disorder (C-PTSD), we will find it difficult to discern past traumas from what is happening in real-time. Our autonomic nervous systems continue to send threat signals, including releasing stress hormones (primarily cortisol and adrenaline) which only worsen our post-traumatic stress symptoms. While these autonomic nervous system responses are adaptive and operating to help us survive,[18] we perceive all is in chaos. We do not know who we are. We do not know how to move forward. Our minds are foggy, our emotions run high and reactive; we are hypervigilant, distrusting, anxiety ridden. Or we are shut down. Depressed. Checked out. Disconnected.

We may become chronically sick with "mysterious" illnesses, isolated, alone, and lonely. We might become afflicted with other maladies, autoimmune or endocrinological in nature—Hashimoto's Thyroiditis, Crohn's Disease, Irritable Bowel Syndrome (IBS), Systemic Lupus Erythematosus (SLE), Myeloencephalitis (ME, also known as Chronic Fatigue Immune Dysfunction Syndrome, or CFIDS), Fibromyalgia, Rheumatoid Arthritis (RA), and Multiple Sclerosis (MS).

As the accompanying symptoms of our threat defenses emerge, we may find ourselves binging on unhealthy foods, withdrawing and avoiding. We may drink too much. Self-medicate with other substances. Distract ourselves with anything that takes us away from present time and our distressed emotions. We cannot sleep. We feel hopeless. We have flashbacks, nightmares, panic attacks, and relational and interpersonal challenges. We view ourselves with judgment: negatively, critically, punitively. We hate ourselves. We blame ourselves. We feel we are bad or not enough. We hide from everyone,

Transfiguration

including and especially ourselves. Yet, to move forward means *embarking* on a transformational healing path that asks us to move through thresholds of returning, as our bell jar cracks, leaving us to face our own inescapable emptiness.

~

Intentional Invitation
Sit down in a quiet space and gently notice one thought, one emotion, and one body sensation you had while reading this theme of Crisis. Write these observations down on a piece of paper. Now, do something that will soothe your body using your five senses: sight, touch, sound, smell, and taste. Here are a few ideas: watch the sun set, listen to relaxing music, bake your favorite dessert, take a warm salt bath, take a walk slowly, practice yoga, work in the garden, look through a telescope at the stars, mow the lawn, make a cup of your favorite tea, or burn a scented candle.

Reverent Reflection
bell jar cracks
shrieking—
decision time

3
EMBARKING

"Behold, I have set before you today life and prosperity, and death and evil."
—Deuteronomy 30:15

Facing our own emptiness is terrifying. To realize that we have a hole inside of us that aches for filling and yet no matter what we fill this hole with, including external things, such as: money, people, cars, big screen televisions, the latest iPhone, homes, pornography, drugs, sex; or things that appease our internal appetites, such as: power, prestige, or position—nothing quite remedies this inner ache deep inside of us. This is because the hole inside is a spiritual one and necessarily needs to be filled with spiritual sources, connecting us to ourselves at the deepest place, where our truest most authentic selves live. It is also about connection with others and connection with something altogether beyond us.

Call it what you may: God. Source. Spirit. The Holy One. The Companion. The Friend. Higher Power. Divine

Transfiguration

Intelligence. The Christ. Yeshua. Divine One. Allah. Nature. Energy. Quantum Physics. Buddha. Beloved. Nothingness. Jesus. Mystery. Nomenclature matters less than the illuminating realization that we are not the center of the universe. There is a presence that is beyond our intellectual grasp. There is something else that we can tap into, especially by coming to know ourselves intimately and discovering who we are most authentically. It is Mystery. The Unsayable. The Nameless.

To embark on a transformational healing path means we make an intentional choice to embark into our interior wilderness, rife with revelations, tumult, trials, and redemption—another threshold of returning. We realize we are at the point where we need to decide how we want to live our lives: to heal or not. Either we stand still, remain stuck, and eventually atrophy from the inside out. Or we step into the unknown with uncomfortable uncertainty, risking all and exposing our most sensitive and uncertain spaces inside to ourselves and others for the first time in our lives. We are ready to take responsibility for our soul-wounds. We are ready to change.

When we choose to embark on a transformational healing path, we do so because we need and want to experience the world as a safe, welcoming, healthy place. We want to connect with ourselves in body and mind, and we want to relate, feel positive, experience joy, feel anchored, and look out on our life with hope and promise. We want to experience love, connectivity, and belonging. We will fill our empty hole once we plumb the depths of our embodied interior landscape, traverse the subtle yet complex geography of our hearts and touch the numinous terrain of our souls. We can only do this, however, if we are in a *safe* space, both neurobiologically and relationally.

~

Intentional Invitation
Write down your answer to this question on a piece of paper: what is one action step I can take today to advance my decision to embark on a transformational healing path? Fold it. Place it where it will be safe. Leave it there for 24 hours. Then return to it. Read it. See if your answer has changed.

Reverent Reflection
O Loving One,
I stand at the door of the unknown afraid.
If I step through it, I cannot go back.
If I stand still before it, I cannot go forward.
I do not know what will come.
Gift me safety.
Gift me trust.
Gift me the grace to say *yes*
to all that lies ahead in uncertainty.

4
SAFETY

"Where there is no wise guidance, the nation falls, but in the multitude of counselors there is victory."
—Proverbs 11:14

We know that trauma disrupts our ability to feel safe physically, psychologically, and emotionally. We struggle with our inability to regulate our nervous systems, as we move in and out of fight, flight, freeze, fawn, and fold (collapse). For the trauma survivor, holistic safety is essential to undertake the transformational healing path. Safety and stability in a collaborative therapeutic relationship are of paramount importance. This relationship is where a trauma survivor will learn how to co-regulate their autonomic nervous system, learn safety cues, and feel safe relationally, psychologically, and biologically.

This relationship is one in which the trauma survivor is unconditionally regarded and accepted just as they are. It is a relationship in which judgment and criticism are absent and relational attunement is present. It may be the first and only relationship in which a person experiences unconditional positive regard[19], acceptance, affirmation, empathy, encouragement, and fidelity. In this context, then, it very well may be the only relationship wherein someone comes to know that they are loved, because love by nature is unconditionally accepting, affirming, empathic, encouraging, and faithful. This relationship is both neuro-biologically and relationally safe—and it is sacred space.

It takes time to re-establish a fundamental sense of safety and trust. In Erikson's psychosocial stages of development,[20] safety and trust are developed early in life. When we experience life traumas, especially developmental and complex traumas, our safety and trust are shattered. So, we need to re-establish a sense of safety, stability, and control over ourselves and our environment. We need to be with others, again and again, with whom we can co-regulate our nervous systems. When trauma survivors are dysregulated, we feel a myriad of emotions, such as feeling threatened, overwhelmed, and distraught with tearfulness, anger, and rage. We might want to fight, kick, or scream; or we feel an urge to run, feeling trapped with severe anxiety. Or we feel paralyzed, numbed out, shut down, and disconnected. We might even collapse becoming immobilized altogether.

We learn how to self-regulate our autonomic nervous systems, as we experience a safe relationship working with a skilled professional, and as we connect with others with whom we feel safe, calm, connected, and accepted. We sense we are safe in a therapeutic relationship through the safety cues we discern, such as: a therapist's facial expression, tone of voice, body movements, and how they speak with us. We learn to feel physiologically safe, as we engage in our ventral vagal state of social engagement and connection. In this state, we are calm, emotionally regulated, socially engaged, empathic, creatively resourceful, curious, and open to connectivity and receptivity. We are in our window of tolerance.

Co-regulating our nervous systems with safety and stability are the necessary nutrients to begin a transformational healing process. Clinicians trained in polyvagal theory and trauma recovery—neuro-based, and somatic-based therapies[21] are optimal therapeutic companions for transforming trauma. We can neither think nor talk our way to our transformational healing. Trauma is an embodied reality that we carry within our blood and bones and brain. Thus, we must engage in bottom-up, body-based, neuro-based trauma therapeutic modalities that attend our somatic, brain-based trauma experiences. Trauma-informed talk therapies are helpful adjuncts to somatic trauma therapies.

It is essential that a trauma survivor feels relationally connected and trusting with their trauma therapist, as they begin to reaffirm safety and trust interpersonally and neurologically. To begin the healing process of transforming our soul-wounding, a trauma survivor who feels safe and is co-regulated will begin to open up and be willing to share who they are, where they have been, and who they are becoming. In time, they will be more able to frame their experiences and explore their autonomic nervous system responses to perceived threats or safety cues in their environment with compassionate curiosity rather than punitive judgment.

They will learn how to be self-compassionate and discover, over time, that change is possible and spiritual renewal inevitable. They will have the capacity to sustain social engagement in their ventral vagal state and learn how to navigate in and out of the sympathetic state (fight, flight), the dorsal vagal parasympathetic state (freeze, collapse), or fawning, which involves both the ventral vagal and the dorsal vagal states—fawning is a type of mimicking of the social engagement, or safety state and, at the same time, it involves disconnecting and disassociating that is characteristic of the dorsal vagal state.[22]

With light filtering in through the cracks of their traumatic soul-wounding, trauma survivors who want to heal will need to muster the courage to search wholeheartedly for a safe therapeutic relationship, in which they may enter the threshold of returning that will carry them deep into the unknown realms of themselves. As they transition into this realm, they may begin to feel *crushed in spirit*.

∼

Intentional Invitation

What does it mean for you to feel safe? I invite you to go outside in nature and select two items. One will represent what it means for you to feel safe. The other will represent what it means for you to feel unsafe. Then place the two items in a sacred space, such as on an altar, side-by-side. Let them be visual representations or symbols of your inner life of safety and threat.

Reverent Reflection

> May I feel accepted
> May I feel seen
> May I feel heard
> May I be safe.

5
CRUSHED IN SPIRIT

*"I had no rose for flinging
save one that drank my tears for dew."*
—Sara Teasdale

We suffer deeply from our soul-wounded places. Shame is at the root of our ruptured selves and takes root in our bodies through our developmental trauma. Shame belief tells us to hide, to lie, to pretend because we feel we are not enough. We are bad. Not lovable exactly as we are. Not attractive. Not brave, not strong, not smart. That we are so utterly defective we must remain isolated, hidden, living our lives in secret self-loathing, and enduring the never-ending internal harsh judgments we levy against ourselves. We are blinded by our shame so much so that even when we are met by love, we can barely withstand how love reflects our true identity and the infinite longings of our hearts. It is too much to bear. We cannot yet meet our true selves. Our shame-based perfectionism and inner critic refuse us this gift and tells us we are undeserving of love.

Transfiguration

The perceived certainties of the distant past fade, as we step into the unknown world of multiple anxieties; steeped in our shame, we awaken to the realization we can no longer carry the burden of feeling unworthy, unloved, and unimportant. We can hardly tolerate being in our own skin or being present to ourselves. We are discouraged and *crushed in spirit*, another threshold of returning. Shame is a primary emotion and toxic shame spirals can catapult us into the dorsal vagal parasympathetic state. This state of dorsal vagal complex, or freeze response, is not necessarily a "bad" thing. It is a survival, protective mechanism that is meant to be short-term.

However, for those of us who grew up living with chronic trauma, abuse, neglect, or stress, it has become our nervous system's default coping mechanism for survival, when our neuroception[23] tells us we are facing a threat that we cannot fight off or from which we cannot flee. In this state, our heart rate, blood pressure, muscle tone, facial features, and social engagement decrease. Our breathing is shallow. Our immune response is lowered; we are low energy and fatigued. Our digestive system is likely to be impacted adversely. We cannot think clearly. We feel isolated, alone, helpless, and powerless. We might feel trapped or that we have no options. We need to conserve our physical and emotional energies, and we may feel unable to get through a day without heroic effort.

This is when we need to honor our body's barometer. If we have little to no energy, then we might be slowed down in basic tasks. We will need to make an extra effort to exercise basic self-care, as we may also experience depressive symptoms, including lethargy, fatigue, loss of appetite or overeating, over sleeping, loss of motivation, sadness, or hopelessness. If we are not yet in a safe therapeutic relationship when we find ourselves *crushed in spirit*, we will suffer from deepening isolation and loneliness. We might find ourselves on the brink of despair.

This is the time we want to "wake up" out of immobilization, dorsal vagal parasympathetic dominance state into our sympathetic state of mobilization, and eventually back into our ventral vagal complex state of social engagement—mindfulness, calmness, curiosity, openness, and connectivity. This might look like shifting from feeling depressed to feeling anxiety. Here are three simple grounding and vagal toning exercises we can use to help us activate ourselves out of dorsal vagal complex into our sympathetic system.

First, using our five senses, it is helpful to look around and name five things you can see, four things you can touch, three things you can hear, two things you can smell, and one thing you can taste. This exercise helps us re-orient to our surroundings. Second, start humming, singing, shouting, or uttering "om" out aloud. Finally, laugh! Watch some stand-up comedy and laugh.

Other ways to exercise our vagal nerve when we are crushed in spirit and experiencing a freeze or shut down, include breathing deeply, such as box breathing,[24] listening to energetic music, practicing yoga, or placing an icepack or cold water on our face or neck. We may notice we have distressed feelings arise initially, and that is to be expected, as we are "waking up" from a state where we were numb and moving into a state of mobilization. As we move through these uncomfortable feelings, we will eventually experience relief and reconnection.

Once reregulated it would be beneficial to reach out to one person where there is emotional reciprocity, someone who helps us feel safe and accepted. This might be a friend, a sibling, a sponsor in a 12-step program, a pastor, therapist, or spiritual director. Someone who accepts us, even and especially when we are having a rough time with symptoms of immobilization or shut down. As we awaken from our state of shut down, again, we may feel distressing emotions, such as anger, fear, anxiety, and even a sense of *darkness*.

~

Intentional Invitation

Take a moment to check in with your breath. What do you notice? Is it shallow, slow? Now check in with your body: what sensations do you feel in your face, shoulders, neck, arms, abdomen, legs, feet? Now, notice the quality of your thoughts. Just gently notice your breath, body sensations, and thoughts. Now, get up and make yourself a cup of your favorite tea or other hot beverage. And sit down and take ten minutes to slowly sip the hot beverage. Do nothing else. Turn off your devices and quietly sit and sip your drink mindfully. See what you notice as you do only this one activity.

Reverent Reflection

I recognize my attachment wounding. I still feel betrayed. Unsafe. Terrified. To blame. I smell the stench of toxic shame, as it fills my whole body and seeps out of my mouth, when I speak or when I freeze again and fail to speak. I see myself acting in ways that do not promote my well-being. No one knows more clearly than I how my life feels like it is teeter-tottering between my false persona and my unknown authentic self.

> I want to change.
> I want to be different.
> I am scared.
> I do not trust.
> I lie to others and myself.
> I know I cannot go on.
> I am *crushed in spirit*.

6
DARKNESS

"How she longed to get out of that dark hall, and wonder about those beds of bright flowers..."
—Lewis Carroll

Encountering darkness is terrifying. We cannot see. Yet our eyes adjust to the darkness, as the poet Emily Dickinson so elegantly states in her poem, "We Grow Accustomed to the Dark." Western culture has often projected darkness as something primarily negative, something we are to fear or avoid. This is only one cultural interpretation. The paradox is, while darkness can be scary and even terrifying, because we are unable to see as we do in the light and we are facing the unknown, darkness is also where hidden life teems.

Consider the flower bulb planted deep into rich soil in November. Long after the bloom on a flowering bulb plant has flourished, about mid-August, as the leaves and flowers wilt, nutrients return to the root of the bulb, acting as a catalyst to begin growing new root systems from which spring blooms will emerge. Have you ever held a fall flower bulb in your hand? It feels like a small ball, a golf ball slightly enlarged. Have you ever cut open a bulb? If so, you would find a myriad of overlaid stems tightly pressed together that, once planted, will break open and stretch deep into the soil, anchoring the plant and setting out strong roots from which they will draw necessary nutrients out of the soil to sustain the bulb.

As winter nears, the bulbs fall asleep, sort of. They enter a half-sleep phase where they begin a dormant period—a dark descent. The bulbs remain the same size and do not produce leaves above the ground. Yet, hidden beneath the darkness of the soil, away from human sight, the bulb is silently growing, stretching its roots, and spreading deeper into the darkness of the soil, resulting in a stronger root system. Winter brings freezing temperatures above ground. The dark rich soil acts as a protector against elements of weather, including frost and freeze damage. The bulb remains forgotten, while the coldness of the soil activates chemical, hormonal changes that support the bulb for its spring growth.

These invisible changes unfold as the days get shorter and the temperatures drop lower. During this half-sleep, or dormant period, the bulb proceeds through the winter months of short days, long nights, and colder, even freezing temperatures, until it has sustained itself for a certain number of chilling days. As the temperatures rise and it continues to undergo hormonal changes, eventually, as if intuitively, the bulb begins to grow towards blooming, as the first greening stems of daffodils, crocuses, and tulips push their way out from the dark soil. The bulb needs both the time to be dormant and wintry weather to gather sufficient energy to put on its riotous show of fresh, colorful blooms in the spring. The bulb cannot bloom without these two components for growth.

Like the bulb planted in the fall, trauma survivors who start down the path to transformational healing of soul-wounding to soul-mending, or transfiguration will enter the fecund, dark soil of their souls (psyche). It is a *dark night of the soul* experience, a purgation, wherein we meet all the wounded, alienated, unwelcomed aspects, facets, or versions of ourselves. We bump up against the orphaned, conflicted, lost, alienated, frightened, shame-based, contradicted and disintegrated parts of ourselves, and with this encounter we experience fear, shame, unworthiness, guilt, punishment, terror, grief, and loss of all that is familiar and safe; we encounter our own violence, despair, self-hatred, neglect, and abuse.

These wounded facets of ourselves call out to us from the wild edges of our embodied interior landscape for love to begin. They are our hidden life—a composite of awe and wonder, grief and sorrow, fear and hope, subsisting beneath the dark soil of our hearts. They have remained dormant for a prolonged period of emotionally chilling days and nights. They have languished, holding life at their roots, while awaiting the nurturing sustenance of our self-compassion, gentle tenderness, and loving-kindness. They have been waiting in dark grace for our *befriending*.

~

Intentional Invitation

In answering the following questions, select one that speaks most deeply to you and journal for 10 minutes. 1. How willing am I to meet myself in my soul-wounding? 2. What do I need practically and spiritually to support me in this dark descent? 3. When was my one companion darkness?

Reverent Reflection

>Into dark night
>tumbling,
>floundering
>I strain my eyes
>All is hidden.
>Into dark night
>watching,
>waiting
>I listen
>There is nothing.
>Into dark night,

Transfiguration

>   heart-fire
>   burning—
>   *holy* longing,
>   my only guide,
>   draws me
>   into the
>   dark cavern
>   of my soul.

7

BEFRIENDING

"Further, on the assumption that there are not several souls, but merely several different parts in the same soul, it is a question whether we should begin by investigating soul as a whole or its several parts."
—Aristotle

We have abandoned wounded versions of ourselves indefinitely in the winter element of emotional frost and the autonomic nervous system chill that accompanies trauma. We have dissociated and sometimes collapsed. We have turned away from our authentic selves in our pain. We have taken flight from our own darkness—the rich soil of our soul-wounding. It is in this dark soil that we can seek healing within a safe relationship, wherein we can begin to transform our broken, fragmented, alienated selves.

We have entered another threshold of returning, the gateway to encountering ourselves as we truly are. As we begin this process of befriending ourselves in our

Transfiguration

soul-wounding, we meet our false self—the *persona* we present to the world. It is the small self, the one our ego defends relentlessly. It is bound up in the pursuit of naked power, status, competition, and ambition. Or, simply put, the illusion of control! Our false selves mask and protect our most fundamentally important human quality—vulnerability. Our false selves rationalize and justify why we ought never be vulnerable.

Vulnerability, however, is the very portal to our inner wilderness. It strips us bare of all that is not authentic. Of all that is performative. Of all that is false. Of all that is fear-based. Of all that is unwilling to risk. Of all that is obsessed with control. It exposes us to ourselves in our utter rawness as we are—and it offers us a glimpse into who we are meant to be and become. It draws us into authentic connection and purpose with ourselves and others. It reveals new layers of meanings in our lives. It brings us to our knees at times; at other times, it gently beckons, draws, and invites us to kneel, unfolding our clenched fists, with palms opened and hands outstretched, offering all we are to something altogether beyond ourselves.

In our vulnerability, we are called to turn towards the wounded aspects of ourselves—our wounded, fragmented collective selves and to listen to what they have to say to us. What do they have to teach us about our beliefs and thoughts? Where are they manifesting in our bodies? How might we attend to their fears, unmet needs, and longing for belonging and love?

The troubling sides of us are spiritual sources of revelation—they are pointers to our deepest desires, needs, and hopes. Our wounded, fragmented facets are sources of revelation, as they provide us with understanding and clarity about our false, maladaptive, performative selves and their unmet needs. In bringing curiosity and compassion to these dimensions of ourselves, they transform into our partners, who help point the way to our most authentic selves, which for some people may be an integrated single self and for others a plurality of selves.

Transformation heals our wounded, fragmented selves by changing the quality of these aspects or facets of ourselves. Our transformational healing is not necessarily about joining the varied facets into one unified whole, as much as it is about radically changing the quality of these facets, so they function operationally as a cohesive whole. Integration of our wounded, fragmented selves, then, is about transforming these various facets of ourselves into aspects that have their needs met—they know they are worthy, valued, and loved.

When we touch our own silent suffering and the fringes of our fragility, as we befriend ourselves in all our wounded aspects or facets, something alchemical happens—we are moved to *surrender*.

~

Transfiguration

Intentional Invitation

Sit down in a quite space and write a letter to a good friend who is suffering and feeling worthless, because they realize they have deeply frightening aspects of themselves, and, therefore, feel unworthy of love. Seal the letter and place it in safekeeping for three days. On the third day, take out the letter and read it aloud replacing your friend's name with your own. Notice with curiosity and compassion what thoughts you have, what emotions arise, and where in your body you feel them.

Reverent Reflection

> May I bow deeply
> to all that lies within me—
> selves unknown, abandoned,
> neglected too long.

8
SURRENDER

"A change, in a change that is remarkable there is no reason to say there was a time."
—Gertrude Stein

Surrender. The abyss of humiliation. Bottomless shame and disgrace. We have condemned ourselves. We have lived with indifference towards ourselves. We have marginalized ourselves. We have abandoned ourselves. We arrive at the point where we recognize whatever we have been *doing* in reaction to our lived experience of trauma, has not worked. We are ruptured. We are in the dark. We are afraid. And we are utterly stuck: we cannot move forward, and we know we cannot go back. We surrender.

Surrendering is not something a trauma survivor does easily, as feeling out of control, experiencing a loss of agency, is at the core of the trauma survivor's soul-wound. Surrender comes only once the trauma survivor has reached a place in themselves, where they can no longer move forward, despite their fear of letting go of whatever perceived control they have. Yet, they absolutely cannot go back. They are at a still point.

In transforming trauma, there is a delicate balance: the trauma survivor must learn to build trust again in a relationship of safety; it is the foundation to rebuild themselves from the inside out. At the same time, the trauma survivor has legitimate fears and good reasons to distrust. Therefore, it is vital to secure a safe relationship in which they can begin the healing process. While this relationship is often that of a professional clinically trained in trauma, it can also be a community of fellow survivors of trauma, or both. To surrender is to let go of our perceived sense of control over ourselves and our environment. It involves letting go of our self-will, which is different than self-determination or moral agency. Self-will rises up from our wounded false, maladaptive, performative selves; self-determination or moral agency rises up from our transforming, unfolding authentic selves. Both self-will and self-determination co-exist in the trauma survivor.

Surrendering assumes we have reached the point where we can see things as they are rather than how we have wanted them to be or believed them to be. This seeing, this clarity of discernment, splinters our illusions. Surrender and acceptance are intimately interconnected—we surrender only once we have accepted our reality. We cannot heal from our traumatic ruptures, our soul-wounds, unless we acknowledge and recognize that we are disrupted, even paralyzed by our lived traumas. Surrender involves leaning into our own life stories and allowing our narratives to carry us by their contours, characters, and conflicts, until we encounter ourselves in a space of acceptance—the beginning of returning to our authentic selves.

Accepting our human condition allows us to meet ourselves as we surrender all that we are at a given moment. We enter our rupture. We meet ourselves in all our disrupted and split-open humanity. We open our palms with outstretched hands offering all that is no longer working in our fragmented lives. This is a *holy* moment when we can enter the threshold of returning named surrender—be present to our wounds and accept that we need healing. We choose to surrender.

Acceptance allows the trauma survivor to breathe in again; surrendering allows for relief to follow as we breathe out. We can think of surrendering paradoxically as both an acknowledgement of our internalized oppression rooted in our embodied traumatic suffering and as an act of freedom, signifying our journey out from our suffering into a place of possibility—a different, transformed, transfigured, renewed life.

One might think of surrendering as offering our "bread of affliction,"[25] or, *Ha Lachma Anya*,[26] in Jewish religious tradition. It is the first passage from the

Transfiguration

Magid section of the Passover Haggadah. The bread of affliction refers to the unleavened bread, or Matzah, uncovered in the Passover Seder, or *Pesach*. It symbolizes both the suffering the Jews endured as slaves in Egypt, and it also points to their freedom in leaving Egypt. Surrendering our *bread of affliction* means we want to be open to possibility.

~

Intentional Invitation

Find a quiet space. Write down the following questions on two strips of paper. Fold the strips and place them in a small bowl. Leave them for 30 minutes. Do something that involves movement of your body—stretching, yoga, Tai Chi, or a brisk walk. After 30 minutes, return to the bowl and select one of the strips of paper. Open it. Read it slowly. Write down your answer. Here are the two questions: 1. What am I afraid of surrendering? 2. What am I gaining by holding onto whatever it is I need to surrender?

Reverent Reflection

>let go
>embrace
>mystery

9
BREAD OF AFFLICTION

"What fate is mine? Who guides or guards my ways, seeing my soul, so lost and ill-betided, burns in your presence, in your absence dies?"
—Michelangelo Buonarroti

Let us consider how our suffering, our hardship rooted in our oppressive states of unhealed trauma, becomes our "bread of affliction." Our enslaved states, where our limbic systems are not yet healed—our intrusive thoughts and dysregulated emotions may torment us, and our depressed or negative moods prevent us from participating fully in our lives. All these variations of suffering and symptoms in PTSD, C-PTSD, and other forms of developmental, chronic, and real-life traumas, become our oppressors.

We are disrupted by the daily vicissitudes of our emotional, mental, and physical soul-wounding. When we surrender, we choose to leave our enslaved lives of psycho-spiritual and physical bondage and enter life fully

Transfiguration

unknown, where we hope to experience freedom. As we begin our own exodus from a life of psycho-emotional traumatic oppression, we are filled with excitement, even euphoria, at first, only to realize as we settle into our newfound life of learning how to co-regulate, attending our embodied sensations, and naming our wounds, we continue to face other harsh realities born out of the uncertainty, unfamiliarity, and hostilities we encounter for having chosen to heal ourselves. Transformational healing is often a threat to those still enslaved in their oppressed, unhealed, traumatized selves. As we leave behind our former selves, we begin to realize all else that we have left behind. Sometimes, we leave behind people whom we have loved, places that we have called home, or things that have defined us. We let go, taking baby steps, learning to trust, little-by-little, sometimes minute-by-minute, as we companion with a skilled professional who guides us on our transformational healing path.

Depending on our attachment style—secure, avoidant, anxious, or disorganized, we may struggle with the inner conflict of our longing to be connected and our survival defense response to push away relational connectivity. We push until out of sheer exhaustion and hopelessness, we reach a place where we choose to let go and trust, while also recognizing our fears, insecurities, distrust, and lack of self-confidence. Still, we choose to open our palms and offer who we are in all our messy, exhausted, survivor selves.

We enter our inner exodus, a wilderness. We begin to plumb the depths of our embodied interior landscape, traverse the subtle yet complex geography of our hearts and touch the numinous terrain of our souls, where we meet ourselves exactly as we are—wounded, ruptured, raw, hidden in darkness, and bruised by the chilly temperatures of our traumas. In this unavoidable encounter with ourselves, we are filled with a growing awareness that we are shedding old skins for new ones. That we have been touched and are being transformed—we have a *change of heart*.

~

Intentional Invitation
What is my "bread of affliction" that has been weighing me down for so long?

Reverent Reflection
> barely spring
> a naked tree—
> expecting

10
METÁNOIA

"Though I get home, how late, how late!"
—Emily Dickinson

Metánoia, or μετάνοια, is a Greek word meaning a change of mind, change of the inner person, or repentance. I will use it here to mean a "transformative change of heart." When we think about the human heart, we associate it with love. All kinds of love: Eros (passionate, romantic), Agape (selfless, universal), Philia (affectionate love, friendship) Philautia (self-love), and Storge (familial love). We might also associate the heart with the mind, or the seat of our consciousness. In Jewish spirituality the heart, *lev*,[27] is considered both a physical organ and the center of a person's thoughts and emotions. It is the seat of one's physical, moral, and spiritual life.

With this latter meaning and context in mind, then, let us consider what a *metánoia*, or change of heart, would mean practically? It might mean changing habits around our daily living and self-care—what we eat, how we sleep, what we do with our time. It might mean changing our friends and relationship with families of origin. It might mean, searching ourselves deeply to discern what our core values are. What does integrity mean? What work we are called to? What do we believe in? Do we have a spiritual connection?

Metánoia is a radical transformation from the depth of our invisible being to our visible personhood. A transformative change of heart is a total reevaluation of every aspect of our lives: body, mind, spirit, and soul. It is an embodied spiritual conversion, a threshold of returning towards our transfiguration. A trauma survivor who has surrendered has already turned their heart—an interior change, or conversion of heart. Now that they have taken the step to let go, they will be faced with another decision: how much do they want to let go? Or more realistically, how much will they need to let go to move their life forward?

How can a trauma survivor begin to deconstruct their insides when they feel so unstable, so emotionally dysregulated? They must establish safety within a nurturing, supportive therapeutic relationship of trust. Over time, that relationship, or container, will serve as the safe space for them to begin their deeper healing journey, or transformation. As they stabilize and trust, for the first time, they will undoubtedly begin to experience an implicit, felt, embodied remembering and, eventually, the ability to let go, detach, surrender, and empty themselves; this will be accompanied by *sorrow, grief, and loss.*

~

Intentional Invitation

Reflect on the following two questions. See which one resonates the most and sit with the question for three minutes. See if you can simply be with the question rather than find answers for it. Notice what comes up for you: thoughts, emotions, body sensations, and images. 1. How do I understand what my heart is? 2. What is the thing I am holding onto that feels like life and death if I let go?

Reverent Reflection

> Perpetually unfolding
> beneath stone and leaf
> and wild earth
> I doggedly fling my hope
> towards the silhouette
> of a self
> still becoming

11
LAMENTATIONS

"A thousand years of grief are packed therein."
—Poet Unknown
Han Dynasty or earlier

Losing someone we love is soul wounding. The world shifts. It is disorienting. We come to realize we are alone. That everything is imbued with a remembrance that fills us with a deep ache. We need to relearn how to be in the world without our loved one. We know intellectually our loved one is no longer here and is gone from our lives; and yet, we also feel or sense our loved one. As if they are still with us, although beyond our grasp. A kind of knowing and unknowing. Losing someone we love brings us face-to-face with our powerlessness. Losing someone we love deeply is especially agonizing when we wake up and realize through our grief, it is ourselves, too, whom we have lost. This realization is when we begin our long weeping.

Grieving is holy soul-work. As wounded trauma survivors we are intimately familiar with grief. We have long carried our lamentations in silence, swallowing our tears, until our grief cries out for expression and healing. We begin our lament. We wail, groan, moan, and feel as if our hearts are being torn from our chests. Our entire body hurts from our life losses. In our lament we recognize our self-betrayal, our deceptive cravings for everything and nothing that will ever satisfy our spiritual hunger, and our forgetfulness that everything we are and make of ourselves counts. We awaken to all the possibilities that have passed us. How we have not lived a life worth living. How we have been on survival for a long, long time. We understand we cannot recapture these losses and we cannot escape change.

As we turn towards our grief, we are called to let go of everything that no longer serves us, even if familiar. This letting go is awful. Embarking on a path that is utterly unworn and unknown is gut-wrenching, particularly if we come to it with hesitant surrender, with fearful acceptance. With humble surrender and grateful acceptance of our vulnerable human condition, however, we become less confused and more willing to embrace our imperfections. We begin to see how the stains of our emotional bruising and palpable physical collapse are the very ingredients that are necessary for the holistic alchemical transmutation of our transfiguration to unfold. We begin to see that everything we have experienced, everything we have failed to experience, everything, everything holds the potential for our deep transformational healing. We become spiritual pilgrims, as we step through the exodus of our bread of affliction. Our lamentations enfold us, and in sobering awe, our eyes glimpse sight of the possibility of a renewed life—imbued with sorrow and song.

It is difficult to fully imagine such a life, however, when we are immersed in our sorrow. We become a requiem. Will our tears ever dry? Will I ever see joy again? Will my body ever feel safe? What can be more serious than this grief? The paradox is a renewed life is always already the place in which we experience our deepest grief. With our tears soaking the land of our soul, washing over our parched psyches, we begin to see more clearly that there is no renewed life without our funeral hymn. We can only lament that which we have come to know well and have loved long. We can only lament life once we reconcile ourselves to its interrogations of our hearts and minds.

Yes. Life interrogates us. It asks us, "How will you spend this day?" And, how we answer will point to how we will spend the whole of our lives. Life asks us, "What do you most fear?" "What do you most love?" "Where are you hurting?" "Where are you healed?" "How willing are you to become whole, transformed, transfigured?" "What can you offer me, I who am called Life?" "How long will you wait before you step into your own authentic skin?" "When will you seek to create something new?" "How long will you hide

Transfiguration

from Love?" "What do you want?" How we respond to Life's persistent questions reveals more than we are often ready to know. Yet, without our entering this interrogation of our hearts and minds, we are unable to articulate and honor our sorrow.

Grief presumes our intimacy with that which we lament. We cannot express sorrow for the superficial. Grief arises from deep beneath the surface of our everyday wakeful selves. Trauma survivors *feel* grief, but until we experience sufficient safety and trust in an affirming relational space in which we are invited to remember and express it, our suppressed grief erodes our ability to co-create the life we know is worth living. Trauma survivors will necessarily have to experience a thousand transmutations of our false wounded selves, before we can embrace our authentic transformed selves.

When trauma survivors are stuck in chronic fight, flight, freeze, fawn, fold (collapse) autonomic nervous system defensive states, we experience feeling as if we are either being swallowed up by our grief or we deny and numb out our interior death song, a dirge. Through a slow march to our funeral hymn, we enter an emotional space where we simply cannot *do* anything more. We must learn how to *be*. This means we must slow down, pause, and *wait*.

~

Intentional Invitation

Choose one of the following questions and journal for as long as words come forth. 1. What are my life's lamentations? 2. How do I need to express my lamentations? 3. How have I answered Life's interrogations?

Reverent Reflection

>In my inconsolable weeping
>my soul offers
>an *Annunciation*—
>a welcoming of the stranger,
>my soul-wound on pilgrimage.
>Tending cracks and chasms,
>and embracing my imperfections,
>I hear a song in
>celebration of my survival.

12
WAITING

"My soul has grown deep like the rivers."
—Langston Hughes

Waiting is like a Sabbath. It asks us to *do* nothing. It invites us simply to *be*. Be present to ourselves in ways that we may never have experienced. To listen deeply to our own inner voice. To honor the rhythms of our bodies: to eat when we are hungry and rest when we are weary. Pray when we are uncertain. Breathe when we think we cannot.

Waiting asks us to reconnect with ourselves, others, and something altogether beyond. Waiting asks us to be willing to let go of our obsession to control. To surrender more. To trust more. To attend more. Waiting asks us to discern the meaning of our in-between times: we are not yet where we hope to be, and we are no longer where we were. We are between selves—the shedding of our false, fear-based, performative self and the anticipation of our unknown, unnamed, authentic self. We are in a liminal space that beckons us to watch and wait expectantly. Attentively. With abandonment. This is counter-cultural to our society that privileges busy-ness and doing.

Waiting necessitates paying attention in a conscious, intentional way. Waiting reorients our attention to the deeper levels of our existence—to extend our gaze and be receptive to all that may come our way. Waiting is a kind of grace that invites us to stop fretting and fixing and to allow the undercurrents of our distress intolerances to manifest so that we can more fully surrender these, too. We cannot wait in a vacuum, though; rather, we need the safety of a nurturing therapeutic relational connection, wherein we are fully accepted exactly as we are in this moment: soul-wounded.

In the safety of this relationship, we begin to feel more stabilized, less out of control, and we learn strategies for staying within our window of tolerance. During this waiting time and in the safety of our therapeutic relationship, we want to manage our triggers, so that we do not get so overwhelmed with panic, anxiety, anger, or depression. So, waiting can be our opportunity to practice safety in our healing.

Waiting means, we must surrender to the process of unfolding. When waiting shows up for us, we are called to greet it with hospitality, even and especially when it appears as an unexpected guest. It *will* appear unexpectedly. Waiting usually visits us when we are least equipped for life—when we hit our low points, when we are least naturally patient and willing to trust, when we feel enormous pressure to "do something." When we feel least hospitable. This is when waiting will come knocking at our door. We are not often asked to wait when things are going swimmingly. There is no need to wait. All seems perfectly in order.

It is when we feel out of order that we most need to wait. This can be exceedingly difficult unless we have both practical and spiritual support. Practically, we need a safe relational space therapeutically; spiritually, we need a contemplative spirituality practice that cultivates our attention: Centering Prayer,[28] Mindfulness meditation, knitting, gardening, birding, cooking, painting, drawing, sculpting, photography, writing, brush painting, pottery, woodworking, running, walking, rock climbing, swimming, singing, or yoga. Some activity that engages our whole being and involves our whole attention. In this way, waiting refines our ability to be in the present moment, see clearly, listen more deeply, and take actions based on a perspective that is unimpeded with our incessant need to control everything.

Waiting teaches us to trust. To receive each moment as the only moment that counts. To be comfortable with uncertainty. Each moment invites us to surrender all our fears, anxieties, past mistakes, present pains, future longings—all of it. Surrender all of it unto something deeply within and simultaneously beyond ourselves. Each moment invites us to receive its unrepeatable mystery. Waiting invites, us to say "yes" to each moment, to each hue of our lives revealing itself to us. In our rupture and darkness—our soul-wounding, we are called, over and over, again and again, to surrender, take exodus of our bread of affliction, enter the gate of our grief, and simply be. Wait. Trust.

Waiting is something we have done in other capacities—we wait for spring as we near the end of winter. Yet sometimes our waiting can feel like an interminable winter. Waiting reveals our hearts longing. It becomes the hidden ground in which the seeds of our growth, stability, detachment, simplicity, silence, connectivity, creativity, curiosity, and celebration take root. At once our human frailty and possibility are held in creative tension, opening a way through a threshold of returning, an experience of grace and mercy, as we *empty* ourselves of all that is not flourishing.

~

Intentional Invitation

What does waiting bring up for me? When have I welcomed waiting? What keeps me from being able to wait?

Transfiguration

Reverent Reflection

If I do not strive
If I do not grasp
If I do not tarry
If I do not hide,
and simply wait,
what
shall
I
become?

13

KENOSIS

*"Two roads diverged in a wood, and I,
I took the one less traveled by,
And that has made all the difference."*
—Robert Lee Frost

Kenosis comes from the Greek word Κενόω, (kenóō), meaning "to empty out." Its meaning in Christian theology refers to Jesus of Nazareth, emptying himself in total humility and with incomprehensible love to assume the human condition as a servant for all of humanity. In Philippians 2:6 we read, "who, though he was in the form of God, did not count equality with God a thing to be grasped but emptied himself, by taking the form of a servant, being born in the likeness of men."

How does this relate to the trauma survivor? A trauma survivor is often operating with inadequate ego development—they are often operating from their false, maladaptive, performative, disrupted, wounded, fragmented selves and not their authentic selves that emerge, heal, and renew only over time with depth of inner transformation. *Kenosis* for the trauma survivor points to an intentional choice to offer their false wounded selves to be radically transformed in search of their authentic transfigured selves.

It is an "emptying" of our former life stories and scripts, so that we can rewrite our renewed ones from a place of healing, strength, and meaning making. By self-emptying I mean we choose to let go of what is and what has been for what can be, for what is possible to emerge. In other words, we are intentionally willing to undergo an *unbecoming* of ourselves as we have been for the *becoming* of ourselves as we can be. Adopting an interior attitude of *kenosis* is about emptying ourselves of all that prevents us from tapping into our most authentic selves—letting go of our attachment to our false wounded selves and ego-centric self-will and becoming wholly receptive to who we might be when awakened to the unseen realities within ourselves.

This offering is a self-emptying of all that impedes us from being and becoming our authentic selves—all that presents distractions, denials, and deflections. *Kenosis*, then, is about the self-emptying of our pretenses, rationalizations, justifications, and explanations, as we begin to experience transformative healing, a transfiguration. Once again, a trauma survivor cannot make this choice unless they feel they are safe, relationally and neurobiologically. So, we need to re-establish a sense of stability, safety, and control over ourselves and our environment. It takes time to re-establish a fundamental sense of safety and trust. However, once a trauma survivor is in a safe relationship, they can begin to build trust slowly.

Kenotic transformation is the emptying of our false self-will and performative self, which are deeply shame-based, and as we empty ourselves of our attachment to these wounded selves, we encounter them, befriend them, learn what they need and want, and how they have functioned to keep us alive. We allow the various aspects of ourselves to teach us; and, slowly, we open ourselves to be fully receptive to the transformational process that brings us face to face with the uncertainty of our authentic self, which for some people may consist of a multiplicity of selves.

Transfiguration is not about unifying our soul fragments into a singular whole; it is about radically transforming our fragments or aspects qualitatively and allowing them to be in a functional, supportive relationship with one another. For some this will be a sense of integration of a synthesized self, and for others it will be a sense of plurality with cohesiveness and clarity.

We empty ourselves of all psycho-emotional distractions and noise, so that we can reconnect with our true self as it emerges revealed, restored, and renewed. *Kenosis* is a process that unfolds over time and in the safety of a therapeutic, trusting relationship and as part of a contemplative spirituality path. The emptying and letting go that I speak of entails attentiveness, engagement, and willingness. This attitude of self-emptying creates the expansive interior space necessary for the roots of our true selves to push deep into the fertile soil of our souls, where chemical and hormonal changes occur beneath the surface, hidden from our waking minds. The self-emptying of all that impedes us from encountering our most true selves is a kind of unbecoming. And, in this unbecoming, this self-emptying process, we grow closer to the presence of the ineffable divine within us, the Infinite, Mystery, or the Divine Indwelling. *Kenosis*, then, becomes yet another threshold of returning, through which we are radically transformed, even transfigured.

Undergoing a transformational process of *kenosis*, self-emptying, gives birth to a renewed spirituality. Like all growth, post-traumatic spiritual growth emerges out of the mud of our painful lived experiences. As we transform our soul-wounding, we gather lived wisdom and an embodied knowing—we are humbled that we survived our original wounding, and we learn how to live transformed lives in the dialectic of carrying both the embodied memory of our soul-wounding histories and an enlivened hope, as we look forward to the promise of a renewed, transfigured life. When self-emptied of all that is inauthentic, spiritual gifts come: wisdom, knowledge, understanding, discernment, counsel, Divine Empathy, compassion, fortitude, service, love, and reverence.

Post traumatic spiritual growth emerges as we transform our soul-wounding and pass through various thresholds of returning, letting go of our false selves as we morph into our truest selves, until we emerge healed, transformed, and transfigured. As we move through a kenotic transformational process, returning to our most authentic self and a spiritual connection with the divine, we learn *self-compassion*.

~

Intentional Invitation
What do I need to empty myself of so that I might flourish?

Reverent Reflection
May I be willing to have an interior disposition of *Kenosis*, of self-emptying, of letting go of all that is standing in the way of living a life worth living, of what is possible, as my authentic self.

14

SELF-COMPASSION

"bell crickets
surround the temple –
the voice of Buddha."
—Ava Dasya Rasa

Compassion comes from two Latin words, *com*, or "with" and *passio*, or "to suffer." Compassion, then, literally means "to suffer with." What does this mean? Self-compassion invites us to sit with our own suffering. It means I am present, here suffering along with myself, my many facets or earlier versions of myself. It means I am not going to self-medicate or flee from my own pain. It is a conscious choice to offer compassion to my wounded, fragmented selves. It requires our ability to sustain the social engagement, or ventral vagal parasympathetic state in our autonomic nervous system. We need to be calm, regulated, connected, curious, creative, and able to hold space for our own distress. It involves empathy rather than sympathy.

Sympathy says, "I'm sorry you are in this situation." It protects one from doing anything to be intimately involved with another. Sympathy is socially acceptable and endorsed, as it is polite, emotionally distant, and safe. It requires little to no real risk of self-giving. Sympathy is cordial and caring—and it keeps us on the surface relationally. Empathy, however, is unafraid to be emotionally involved in the messiness of our human condition. It offers intimate help, as it is rooted in love and engages us at our depth. Compassionate empathy is the invisible connection to our vulnerability made visible by our extending ourselves to one another and ourselves wholly with care when we are suffering.

Compassion towards our wounded selves says, "I am here for you." "You matter." "I will protect you." "I will care for you, comfort you, and love you." "You are safe now." Self-compassion transforms our ruptured and fragmented selves into healed aspects of our whole, authentic self. We can more easily attend the multiple wounded versions or facets of ourselves with self-compassion, even though we are often unable to show this same self-compassion to our "whole ruptured self." Our self-loathing and shame keep us rooted in our trauma narratives. Being mindfully engaged with our wounded facets, however, allows us to attend earlier versions of ourselves with deep kindness and care. Transforming trauma is intimately connected with self-compassion.

Transfiguration

Self-compassion is about giving ourselves grace. It is showing ourselves kindness when we are suffering. It requires both courage and vulnerability. It means I treat myself with respect. It means I am ethically bound to do no harm or injury to myself. It is acknowledging the inner critic in our head—that voice that repeatedly plays the same old judgmental, shamed-based script: "I am unworthy. I am a failure. This is all my fault. I cannot do anything right. I am worthless. I am stupid. Something is wrong with me. I am bad!" That voice that keeps us stuck. Our inner critic is shame-based and fear-based. Self-compassion's voice sounds like this: "I am not perfect, and I am loveable just as I am. I am worthy. I deserve kindness and love. I am allowed to make mistakes. I am smart. I am brave. I am good. I am becoming my authentic self."

Self-compassion knows we are ruptured, in the dark, surrendering, lamenting, waiting, emptying, and transforming—and it attends all our imperfections and unwanted facets of ourselves with open curiosity, radical acceptance, prayerful patience, caring courage, and unconditional love. It offers a healing salve to our wounded soul. It listens, watches, prays, sits in silence, and believes through our suffering. It is not a polite, emotionally safe, and distancing gesture of, "I'm sorry you are suffering." Rather, it is a brave, emotionally intimate act of love, "I am here for you. I am not leaving you." Self-compassion embraces us without limit. It asks,

"How can I support you?" "How can I best love you in this moment of suffering?"

Self-compassion is showing ourselves the same quality of kindness that we show our friends. Self-compassion attends our most basic needs for food and rest and play and love. It allows us to practice self-soothing and self-care. It gives us permission to dream, to succeed, to fail, to rise, to love ourselves no matter what. In this we preserve our dignity and worth.

As we pass through the threshold of returning named self-compassion, we learn how to embrace ourselves in all our soul-wounding and how to simply be with ourselves in our full humanity, as we journey towards our authentic self, hidden in the numinous terrain of our soul, our embodied being. When we practice self-compassion, we are both humbled and inspired that we are spiritual yet mortal creatures, pulsating stardust, *enfleshed*—flesh and blood, with beating hearts.

~

Intentional Invitation
What action step can I take today to show myself self-compassion?

Reverent Reflection
May I show myself kindness in my moments of suffering.
May I give myself grace when I feel unworthy.
May I lean into self-compassion when I enter my woundedness.

15
ENFLESHED

"The man's body is sacred, and the woman's body is sacred;
No matter who it is, it is sacred;"
—Walt Whitman

The saying, "We are not human beings having a spiritual experience. We are spiritual beings having a human experience" has been attributed to Teilhard de Jardin, SJ, the 20th century mystic, philosopher, and paleontologist. To be human is to be enfleshed, incarnational, embodied. We are blood and bone and marrow and sinew and skin. We are hearts with atriums and ventricles and brains with neurons and neural networks. We are cells and systems. We are our circulatory, respiratory, skeletal, nervous, and digestive systems.

As trauma survivors we get overwhelmed in our bodies easily and often feel lost. We struggle with depression and anxiety and panic. Our bodies get exhausted, depleted, agitated, numb, and shut down.

We cannot feel our own bodies. We are detached, disconnected, and dissociative. We yearn for wholeness and health and strive; yet we stumble, fall, and give up. We feel enraged and sad and hopeless and defeated. We know we are wounded in our bodies, and we hunger for healing.

We know our bodies are inscribed with our stories of pain and betrayal and abandonment from family and sexual violence and society's oppressions. From societal indifference and insensitivity. From our own inability to love ourselves. Our trauma stories of abuse, neglect, and addiction are carried in our cells and atoms and nerves and synaptic impulses. Trauma is not stored in our rational thinking mind but in the most primitive part of our brain and in our bodies, the limbic system. Our limbic system is situated in our midbrain above our brain stem. Our brains change and our whole self is altered from our traumatic stress responses.

Trauma survivors often cannot feel parts of their bodies. Our senses and sensory experiences are dulled or diminished altogether. This is especially true for those of us who have survived developmental trauma which is connected to our attachment wounds. We lose our sense of relational connectivity and embodied attunement. We experience the world as a dangerous, threatening, fearful place, which is why it is central to establish relational and neurobiological safety for the trauma survivor. For some of us, this might well be the first and only time in our lives that we have experienced what it is to feel safe, accepted, affirmed, validated, even celebrated just as we are, wherever we are, in whatever stage of healing we are.

Trauma impacts several brain structures; three important ones are: the Amygdala, Hippocampus and Pre-Frontal Cortex. The amygdala is the emotional and instinctual, or fear center, and it is involved in our threat responses. It also plays a supportive role in our memories during high stress and trauma events. Our hippocampus is the center responsible for our recall memory but shrinks when we experience a traumatic stress response. Encoding of memories is disrupted. This impacts our ability to distinguish between past and present trauma events, as well as our ability to remember certain aspects of a trauma event. Our Pre-Frontal Cortex regulates our executive faculties—our ability to think logically, plan, organize, make decisions, focus, attention regulation, and concentration. It also is involved in our narrative memories.

Our brains are altered when we are faced with a trauma or perceived threat or danger. When we experience the sense of being overwhelmed by an experience, our limbic system—responsible for detecting threats and responding to them—gets activated, shifting into automatic threat or defense reflexes: fight, flight, freeze, fawn, or fold (collapse). It is also involved in encoding memories and our emotions. Our amygdala secretes stress hormones and neurochemicals (primarily adrenaline and cortisol) that signal threat, and our pre-frontal cortex, or frontal lobe is affected. Our pre-frontal cortex becomes compromised impacting our ability to function as we would otherwise. Sometimes this is referred to as the pre-frontal lobe going "offline." This looks like our ability to make basic decisions, ask for help, or practice basic self-care is disrupted. We are operating on autopilot or practiced survival reflexes. During traumatic events, studies show that the part of our brain called Broca's area, which is responsible for speech, has diminished activity.

Transforming trauma involves tracking our body sensations, along with our thoughts and emotions. We notice how we feel inside ourselves—our felt sense, or the interoceptive part of our brains. It also involves engaging in limbic system trauma therapies that can access, discharge, process, and resolve the physiological and neurobiological signature of trauma in our bodies. We carry our traumatic experiences literally inside our skins until we transform them. As much as our brains and bodies are impacted adversely by trauma, our brains and bodies also have the resiliency and capacity to heal and transform. Our brains are highly adaptable because of neuroplasticity—the brain's ability to create new neuro connections or pathways, thereby helping us to rewire and retrain our brains, as we undergo transformational healing that reverses the effects of trauma.

Transforming traumas in our bodies is not about understanding cognitively, as much as it is about restoring our nervous systems and brains. Therefore, engaging in brain-based, body-based, trauma therapies is vital. Engaging in supportive adjunctive therapies can be of immense value in tapping into our embodied wisdom and soul-care. In addition, participating in body-based movements, such as: Yoga, dance, Tai Chi, qigong, singing, chanting, humming, and breath exercises prove to be avenues for regulating and stabilizing our nervous systems.

As we attend to our incarnational histories of trauma, we begin to awaken to the possibility that we can be comfortable in our own skins. With restoration of relational, neurobiological, and embodied connections with ourselves and others in a safe context, over time through transformational trauma therapy and recovery, something magical happens: we find ourselves alone with ourselves and comfortable in the *solitude* of our own skins.

~

Intentional Invitation

What are three thoughts that I am having? What are the three emotions accompanying these thoughts? Where in my body do I feel these emotions?

Reverent Reflection

I have been so cut off from my body sensations for decades. To begin to feel again is scary and exciting. I did not realize how long I have gone without connecting with my body sensations—tightness in my chest, heaviness in my shoulders, eyes stinging, throat burning, head aching. It is as if I am awakening for the first time to my own embodiment.

I want to feel and connect and be free of the pain I have carried inside my skin for so long. I want to feel light and free. I want to relate to myself in this body. Be incarnationally connected. May I turn towards my embodied pain and simply be with it with compassionate curiosity.

16
SOLITUDE

"I never found the companion that was so companionable as solitude."
—Henry David Thoreau

Solitude is not loneliness. Loneliness shows up in two ways: toxic loneliness and healthy loneliness. Toxic loneliness is the existential reality that we are tragically alienated from our most authentic selves. That we are estranged from our interior life. We feel hollow inside. We feel spiritually impoverished. We are disconnected from who we are in truth. We are unaware of our soul-self. We are soul-wounded. This type of loneliness can feel like a self-absorbing emptiness. When we are toxically lonely, we often seek to be soothed from outside of ourselves. Toxic loneliness often breeds in the barren ground of fear, whereas healthy loneliness thrives in the fertile ground of love. Healthy loneliness emerges out of our connection with our authentic selves—when we yearn for connection with others. We long to share our truest selves with others in a genuine relationship of mutual affection and reciprocity. Healthy loneliness is connected to solitude. Toxic loneliness emerges when we have not plumbed the depths of our embodied interior landscape, traversed the subtle yet complex geography of our hearts and touched the numinous terrain of our souls.

Solitude knows us intimately as it is relationally sustained by love. Its capaciousness permits us to bear inner witness to ourselves as we truly are. In solitude we become filled with awareness of our own mystery—the hidden intimacies of our lives. Many trauma survivors exist in some form of toxic loneliness. Those who have sufficiently healed and transformed their soul-wounding into soul-mending, or transfiguration, however, are able to spend time alone with themselves. They are thrivers, enjoying their own company and discovering what lies covered beneath the surface of their false self. One cannot spend time in solitude easily if one has not encountered their internal ruptured soul-wounding. A trauma survivor who continues to live out of their deepest soul-wounds experiences a piercing loneliness that bleeds into every aspect of their lives that are lived on the surface.

Part of our mourning process as trauma survivors is to encounter ourselves in our open woundedness, grieve the unspeakable losses of earlier versions of ourselves, and begin to make meaning and value out of our ruptures as we reconnect with ourselves and others. In this encounter of ourselves, we begin to enter a relationship with our authentic selves. We learn to be present, to attend, and to listen. We learn self-compassion and self-love. We do so in solitude. We do so by being present to ourselves. Learning how to be present is tricky for the trauma survivor. It is a practice that must be cultivated with trauma-sensitivity; or a survivor could easily slip into emotional dysregulation, panic, anxiety, and re-traumatization.

Therefore, when a trauma survivor begins to practice being mindfully present, which is a spiritual practice of intentionally paying attention in present time without judgment, they would benefit to do so in a safe, therapeutic relationship with someone who is trauma-trained and who has a sensibility of trauma and spirituality. This is because entering solitude is, paradoxically, a spiritual path to connecting with ourselves, others, and the whole of creation. We cannot experience the depths of our own soul or with life itself without moments for recollection, recharging, and restoration in body, mind, spirit, and soul.

In solitude, we awaken to our own thoughts, emotions, and body sensations. We observe how we move through the day and night. How we experience internal and external triggers. How we dissociate from ourselves. How we return, repeatedly, to the chronic stress patterns that keep us disempowered. Solitude teaches us the power of silence, stillness, and surrender. In solitude we connect with our hearts—our deepest desires and longings. We encounter ourselves with a depth that is not possible when we are immersed in the marketplace—a cacophony of noise and distraction.

We begin to get a glimpse of the mystery of our own lives and of life itself. We tap into wonder, creativity, curiosity, courage, respect, resilience, our most authentic voice, our soul. When we choose solitude, we experience both *kenosis*, an emptying out of all that impedes connection with our authentic selves and the divine, and *plentitude*, a filling up of our insides with a sense of abundance, awareness, and awe. We become aware of what German theologian and philosopher Rudolf Otto called, the holy terrifying mystery, or *"mysterium tremendum,"*[29] within us and through the created natural world. This awareness or consciousness is a vital awakening for the trauma survivor.

As we transform our traumas, there will be seasons that call us to be alone with ourselves, to be in solitude. It is important to detach from the busyness of the world to be able to attune to our own natural rhythm and pace. To rest the body and mind and heart. To slow down and attend to our insides with grace. To carve out time and provide the space to be with ourselves free from the incessant noise and demands of our lives. As trauma survivors we might avoid taking this time, because it is so uncomfortable to be with ourselves initially. Trauma prevents us from being present. We are absent, either frozen in the past or ruminating about the future. We do not want to be present in our pain. We have distress intolerance even and especially for ourselves because we carry so much pain and discomfort in our bodies and minds. It is essential that as we undergo our transformative healing, we take small steps towards cultivating solitude.

One way to begin to be alone with ourselves is to set aside 5 to 10 minutes in the still hours of dawn in the early morning and at the quieting hours at dusk in the evening to unplug from our devices and all distractions. Little by little, we build in more time alone until eventually we can unplug for an entire day. Or even a weekend. Over time, with habitual practice, we can elect to take what I call a "hermit" day, where we unplug from the outside world: we do not engage our phones, computers, or other electronic devices. We can take a Sabbath, a day of rest. Or we can continue our work in solitude and silence. It is only in solitude that we experience and connect with an interior space where we can begin to experience *holy listen*ing.

~

Intentional Invitation
What am I afraid of discovering if I take time to be alone with myself? What do I need to be able to spend time alone with myself? How willing am I to build in 5 to 10 minutes a day to be alone with myself?

Reverent Reflection

In solitude,
my soul speaks.
Beyond my soul-wounding,
it reveals who I have always been,
and who I am becoming.
Solitude gifts me
with consciousness
of self and
a connection with others
and the Infinite.
In solitude I enter
the depth of my soul.
I enter Mystery.

17
HOLY LISTENING

"Holy listening is soul listening."
—Ava Dasya Rasa

Obedire, the Latin word for "obey," means to listen to or to pay attention to. *Holy* listening honors what we pay attention to with the ear of our heart.[30] With our whole being. We must be willing to empty our hearts of the busyness and chatter of our lives and our world. Empty comes from the Latin *vamus*, or "to leave or abandon." We consciously choose to abandon all that prevents us from listening and paying attention. When we listen with the ear of our heart, as St. Benedict wrote in his rule for life[31], we listen with our whole being—our body, heart, mind, intellect, memory, will, spirit, and soul. The heart is the source from which we love and from which we serve Love itself. Our heart is the most powerful of all our organs, as it pumps our very lifeblood, contracting regularly and continuously pumping blood into our bodies and lungs. Our hearts are the ground of our vulnerabilities.

When we listen with the ear of our heart, we listen to the very blood of our hearts. We pay close attention. We attend deeply to ourselves and others. To listen in this way, we must be still; we become silent, so silent we can hear the tiniest of whispers. Sometimes we listen with our stilled minds and other times with our slowed breath. As we listen more deeply, we become more vulnerable. To listen with the ear of our heart, then, we are willing to be brave and honest and open; we are willing to enter the chamber of our heart with a desire and decision to bare our soul, bringing our embodied self in all its humanity before Mystery. In this transformational healing process, we recognize we are becoming Mystery, as we allow the Unsayable to touch our hearts and heal our wounds. Listening with the ear of our heart, a threshold of returning, then, is inescapably a transfiguring experience.

In the 1952 posthumous compendium of writings, *Gravity & Grace,* Simone Weil, French philosopher and activist, wrote about attention and prayer.[32] Listening with attention, with the ear of our heart, is like contemplative prayer—it centers us down to the still point[33] of our interior world, deep into the *desert* of our souls.

~

Intentional Invitation
Find a quiet space and either sit in a chair or on a cushion and practice listening with the ear of your heart—deeply, single-mindedly, stilled. What do you notice?

Transfiguration

Reverent Reflection

I am the water pooled in the reservoir
of tears stilled inside your broken heart.
I am the element that runs over the
hard stone of this hallowed place.

18
DESERT WILDERNESS

"But in the loneliest desert happens the second metamorphosis: here the spirit becomes a lion; he will seize his freedom and be master in his own wilderness."
—Friedrich Wilhelm Nietzsche

The Greek word, *érimos,* ἐρημος, means, "desert or wilderness." We each have an interior desert. And some of us literally live in the desert. Living in the high desert is at once thrilling and threatening. The desert is a place that beckons us with its subtle, nuanced beauty, while also bewildering us with its insistence on revealing everything at its core. It compels us to listen deeply. It is a place of spiritual encounter. The desert wilderness of our soul is a metaphor, a threshold of returning, that points to the transfiguring process of transforming trauma. The desert is not a place for surfacing life. It is a place that will cut to the depth of us and all that is beneath the surface. It is wild, untamed, naked, vulnerable, and real. It is where we sharpen our ability to listen deeply, to see

Transfiguration

deeply, and to be present fully. It is sacred space wherein we encounter our demons and the divine.

I recall making a Lenten retreat in a monastery in the high desert of Northern New Mexico in March. The New Mexican high desert holds a concealed beauty amidst its sagebrush, Chamisa, tumbleweed, grasses, and bramble in the dust of March winds. March is an in-between time. A time of anticipation of what is not yet here and a time of letting go of that which is ending. A time pregnant with possibility. At this time of year, at first glance, the desert seems barren, monotone, and even desolate. However, upon seeing deeply, the desert's concealed beauty is revealed—raw, stripped, and exposed. All is exposed. The desert is in transition; it is nearing a new season. Its colors, while muted, are showing hints of fresh green and there are the occasional clusters of deep green conifers that bear witness to life in the high desert. The radical stark, bare beauty of the desert invites our heightened attention to this visible world, deepening our longing for something called renewed life.

If we slow down and pay close attention, and listen with the ear of our heart, we will hear the stirrings of our transformational growth beneath our surface. We cannot rush the birth of our spring. We must allow it to come in its own time. Our interior desert places call us to see, to listen, and to pay attention: Off in the distance, mountains loom and peaks point to the heavens with the glint of showered sunlight piercing thick puffs. The skies are turbulent, threatening rain from the gray swollen clouds drifting slowly across the expansive desert skies. Tall jack rabbits sprint over the vast wide-open space that is also home to cottontails, roadrunners, rattlesnakes, and coyotes. Rocks and earth, dry and dusty, and cracked and solid, merge with the ever-moving horizon. We can hear the call to silence and solitude.

We come to our interior desert places to be alone and to listen with the ear of our heart much like Jesus did, when the Spirit led him into the desert for forty days and forty nights. Yet, as we know from this living story, Jesus encountered anything but sheer silence. Jesus fasted for forty days and forty nights. He was hungry. Then the tempter came to him three times, challenging and taunting him. Three times Jesus refused the illusory temptation of exercising power and control over. Instead, Jesus rebuked the tempter, telling him to flee! And angels came and attended to him.

Our interior desert is a hallowed space that invites us to be still, to be silent, and to listen. If we bend the ear of our heart to attend, we, like Jesus, are brought closer to the land of our authentic selves, where we come face to face with all versions of our wounded, fragmented selves. There is no hiding in this desert, no escaping what we must confront within ourselves. There is no one and nothing to blame for anything. This is a primordial silence and space for wild encounters. We, like the desert, are stripped bare, made naked, raw, vulnerable, and exposed to ourselves in the presence of something altogether beyond.

In traversing the geography of our hearts, we awaken to the realization that we have turned away from our deepest longings and desires out of an inability to tolerate anything that is distressing, or anything we perceive as distressing or threatening. We realize we have been indifferent towards ourselves, even eclipsed ourselves, darkening parts of our authentic identities, compelling them to lay dormant, waiting for us to listen with the ear of our heart. These desert places inside us have been calling out to us to turn our whole attention towards them and to listen. We know intuitively when we do, we will never be the same. At some point we are faced with a choice: we can choose to stay stuck in our wounded, ruptured narratives; or we can choose to transform and undergo a *Kintsugi* process, allowing our gold cracks to illuminate our resilience and beauty.

~

Intentional Invitation

What would happen if I stopped running, stopped fighting, reconnected, and listened with the ear of my heart to the desert wilderness inside of me? What are my fears in turning towards and listening to the wounded, fragmented versions of myself?

Reverent Reflection

In a world saturated with chatter,
I have come to the desert wilderness
to be immersed in silence—
to listen with the *ear of my heart*.
I am here, standing at a threshold,
between the porch and altar of my soul.

19
KINTSUGI

"The refining pot is for silver, and the furnace for gold"
—Proverbs 17:3

Kintsugi is a Japanese word meaning *kin* (gold) and *tsugi* (join).[34] Kintsugi is the centuries-old art of repairing broken ceramic or pottery with tree sap lacquer dusted with powdered gold or painted with liquid gold. In the practice of *Kintsugi*, real gold or gold mica powder is used, as well as composites of zinc, copper, and brass. The once broken object is transformed into a precious, beautiful, strong, resilient piece of art to be treasured. The redeemed piece exposes its flaws which are enhanced by gold.

Kintsugi is a threshold of returning, a transformational healing path that invites us to fill in the cracks in our wounded souls with the gold of transfiguration that gives birth to our authentic selves. What is this gold? The "gold" that mends our wounded pieces is the fire of our deepest longings and desires emerging from our authentic selves, resurrecting from the ashes of our traumas. This gold fills in our hairline cracks, broken segments, missing pieces, rough surfaces, scarred markings, and yawning chasms. It joins our edges, one to another, as it creates a seamless integration of our shattered selves. We become a new creation through the rejoining of our splintered selves, our own unique *Kintsugi* process of transformation and transfiguration.

Gold glint becomes the thread of transforming our soul-wounding to soul-mending, or transfiguration. This gold repair restores the overall integrity of our human vessel. The *Kintsugi* process signals our resilience and strength. The gold illumines our dignity and worth. This process echoes the Zen philosophy of *wabi-sabi*[35] or seeing beauty in flaws and imperfections. It invites us to embrace our imperfections wholeheartedly. Other Japanese notions that are symbolized by this art form include *mottainai*[36], or the expression of regret when something is wasted, and that of *mushin*[37] or the acceptance of change. As we accept the invitation to change through our *Kintsugi* process of repair, restoration, and renewal, we come to genuinely accept and appreciate our imperfections, knowing that nothing we have undergone is wasted in the transfiguring process.

When we decide we want to heal our soul-wounds, we enter a threshold of returning, the passage of *Kintsugi*—the beautifying of our fissures and fragments with the gold of transfiguration that breathes new life into us.

Transfiguration

How does a trauma survivor access and harness this gold? It emerges as part of the mystery that unfolds within the therapeutic relationship—and when a trauma survivor spends time alone in solitude, silence, and stillness, listening with the ear of their heart. In the sacred safe space and in dialogue with a trauma therapist, who is present and listens with the ear of their heart, a trauma survivor begins to gather the gold necessary to repair the broken pieces of themselves. Likewise, in silence, solitude, and stillness our own gold surfaces out of the depths. Like all art practices, the *Kintsugi* of our transfiguration takes time and attention and *presence*.

~

Intentional Invitation

How do I relate to my wounded self? How willing am I to be repaired with the gold of my own deepest desires and longings?

Reverent Reflection

Gold is a symbol of what we become when we are immersed and transformed in the mystery of our soul-wounded selves. Little by little, slowly over time, the dross of our broken, bleeding lives is burned off in the fire of our deepest longings and desires—a hidden abyss. In transforming trauma, we welcome our unexpected authentic self as we return home by another road.

20
PRESENCE

"We convince by our presence."
—Walt Whitman

Trauma survivors have difficulty being present. We feel disconnected emotionally and physically. Sometimes, this is because we are practiced in an autonomic nervous system freeze or fold (collapse) response. Other times, it is because we are emotionally dysregulated. Much of the time, we are unable to hold space for our own distress, let alone that of others. As we undergo transformational, transfiguring healing of our soul-wounding to soul-mending, we learn how to *be* with ourselves. We benefit most from working with a professionally trauma-trained therapist who can guide us, as we learn how to expand our window of tolerance, become emotionally regulated, and offer ourselves compassionate curiosity rather than critical judgment.

So as to yield optimal results, we want to establish a therapeutic relationship with a keenly skilled trauma therapist who is capable of being fully present. While we may be unable to practice presence ourselves in our soul-wounding, we certainly can discern when another person is absent psycho-emotionally though present physically. It is of no support to us if a therapist is unable to hold space for both their own and their client's distress. A trauma survivor co-regulates their autonomic nervous system with that of the trauma professional. So, it is vital that the trauma therapist is regulated and able to hold space for another's distress, ranging from mild to acute. Most importantly in the transformational, transfiguring healing process is for the client to be in a relational space, biologically and interpersonally, where they are unconditionally accepted, affirmed, validated, and encouraged.

A trauma therapist who is fully present and who listens with the ear of their heart will mindfully follow the pace of their client, the survivor, acknowledging and validating with empathy, as they begin to gain a renewed sense of autonomy and identity. A trauma therapist who is present and who listens with the ear of their heart will both set appropriate boundaries with their client and support their client by reaffirming them as the expert of their own lived experiences. Moreover, a trauma therapist who is present and who listens with the ear of their heart will teach practical skills and strategies to their client, so they can learn how to stay in their window of tolerance and how to self-regulate. This involves learning coping skills to manage triggers, so they do not have to suffer unnecessarily from panic, anger, anxiety, and depression.

Trauma-Sensitive Mindfulness, as taught by trauma professional, writer, and educator, David A. Treleaven, PhD,[38] is one way to enhance our capacity to stay in our window of tolerance. Learning how to be present in this moment and pay attention without judgment can be a path for distress tolerance and self-acceptance, so long as this is done with trauma sensitivity. Another way we can be supported is engaging in somatic exercises,[39] which help to re-regulate a person emotionally and ground them. Somatic Experiencing™ and Somatic-Attachment are especially supportive somatic-based trauma therapies for trauma survivors of Chronic Trauma and C-PTSD. These somatic therapies focus on the body and its internal sensations and tracking physical sensations as they correspond with emotions. The goal is to modify the body's stress-related trauma responses.

Once a trauma survivor is in a safe relationship, they can begin to rewire and reset their autonomic nervous system. A trauma therapist who is present and who listens with the ear of their heart will help the trauma survivor to recognize which of their defense strategies and behaviors are the result of the neurobiology of trauma—the autonomic nervous system's fight, flight, freeze, fawn, fold (collapse) mobilization and immobilizations responses. A trauma-sensitive therapist will help their client understand that trauma responses are not their fault. Autonomic nervous system reactions are the brain's way of protecting the person so that they can survive a trauma. If a client's body freezes in the face of a perceived or actual threat and they experience emotional shut-down or dissociation, even in small ways, these are autonomic nervous system defense reactions and not the result of their own cognitive faculties or a moral choice, even though the client may describe feelings of shame and guilt.

As we work with a trauma therapist, who is skilled in supporting us learn how to increase our distress tolerance and transform our trauma somatically, we will learn to be emotionally and physically present to ourselves and others, even and especially in distressing situations. A trauma therapist who is present and who listens with the ear of their heart is companioning us, the trauma client, in a profoundly transformative, transfiguring healing process that leaves both participants forever changed. The therapeutic relationship is a sacred relational space where two souls meet—they are safe, connected, and transformed. It is a relationship in which there is spaciousness enough for relational engagement that includes both uncomfortable and comfortable *silence.*

~

Intentional Invitation

What do I need from my "safe" person—therapist, sponsor, or spiritual director?

Reverent Reflection

>May we enter a relationship
>of radical openness, inclusivity,
>mutuality, generosity,
>presence, and lovingkindness.

21

SILENCE

"Silence is the soul's lover."
—Ava Dasya Rasa

Silence is the soul's lover. Beloved. Spouse. Stillness and solitude are the twin companions to silence. Silence is the antidote to the incessant noise of our consumer-driven marketplace. It offers a medicinal salve for our whole self that has become bound up in the onslaught of frenzied chatter in our culture. It opens a space inside us where we can listen with the ear of our heart. The *hesychast*, the one who has attained inward silence, listens deeply.[40] Silence is not the mere absence of noise. Rather, it is the presence of our full, embodied attention and listening.

To be still and silent, we need to feel safe and regulated. Trauma survivors who have not transformed their soul-wounding often find silence intolerable. So that trauma survivors can benefit from the gift of silence, they will have to reach a place in their transformational journey, wherein they are able to sustain their emotional and bodily regulation. At this stage in the transformation process, they can tolerate some distress and they are practiced in some mindfulness or another contemplative practice sufficiently to pay attention in the moment with compassionate curiosity rather than critical judgment.

We live in a world besieged with noise, chatter, busyness, and consumerism. We live in a world spinning so fast that we can barely take a moment to breathe. We need to be intentional about cultivating silence in our otherwise stimulated lives. This means we will need to be willing to practice being still. An attitude of willingness to create new habits, practices, and routines is optimal. When we begin this new way of moving through our days and nights, we may feel uncomfortable at first, even though we have established a sense of safety and emotional regulation therapeutically. Ours is a society saturated with stimulation, and to practice stillness is not only counter-cultural but also a form of radical self-care. To begin, we might consider setting aside ten minutes at the threshold times of the morning and evening to be still. While interior stillness can be experienced even as we are active externally, this ability comes only after many, many hours of practicing stillness and silence.

We cannot know who we are at our depths unless we slow down, breathe, pause, and become still in silence and solitude. Silence allows us to listen with the ear of our heart to the depths of our desires, our longings—and everything we have not wanted to hear. Transforming trauma means we shed our old skins, our old attachments, and transform our old wounds—through this metamorphosis, we emerge from our false, wounded selves more connected to our true, authentic selves. Oftentimes, we emerge with newfound purposes; we discover gifts, and we tap into possibilities of how we might re-enter our community and serve, using the wisdom and knowledge gathered through our transformational healing process.

Transforming trauma necessitates an intentional change in how we relate to ourselves in our mind, using Mindfulness or contemplative meditation, such as Centering Prayer. In our body we learn how to identify our sensations and how to ground ourselves using somatic and vagal toning exercises; in our spirit we learn how to regulate our emotional life and energies, and in our soul, we ignite a knowing that we did not possess when we were active in our trauma stories. Indeed, it is a transfiguring process: our wounded identity morphs into a renewed self. The silence of our interior desert wilderness is a foundational necessity for us to access dimensions of our inner life that remain unknown, until we get still and are alone and silent.

Silence invites us to get still in solitude, to listen with the ear of our heart, and to begin to rewrite the trauma narratives of our lives. Silence reveals that we *can* pass through the threshold of returning to encounter silence, stillness, and solitude—intricately interwoven elements necessary for us to undergo this transformation, our transfiguration. We cannot have silence without also having stillness and some measure of solitude.

As we grow with consciousness and awareness of our embodied interior landscape, we become less attached to the external objects and activities and frenzies of our world. We become grounded, our discernment becomes more acute, and we tap into a multitude of spiritual gifts: acceptance, compassion, Divine Empathy, knowledge, wisdom, discernment, understanding, mercy, lovingkindness, and reverence. We engage in prophetic seeing, knowing, and announcing to the world new ways of being. A transfigured way of being. A way of *forgiveness*.

~

Intentional Invitation

Choose one of the following and Journal 1. What arises in me when I think about being silent? How willing am I to integrate 10 minutes in the morning and evenings to be silent? What keeps me from practicing silence? 2. Reflect on the following haiku:[41]

> after silence
> a monk
> wakes up
> the bell

Reverent Reflection

May I enter the wordless place inside me, where my only desire is to know myself and to welcome my becoming.

May I listen to the silent music of my soul.

May all that is hidden beneath the silence of the stillpoint, reveal itself—out of the depths.

22
FORGIVENESS

"I don't write this letter to put bitterness into your heart, but to pluck it out of mine. For my own sake I must forgive you."
—Oscar Wilde

What role does forgiveness play in transforming trauma? Let us consider the distinction between forgiveness and reconciliation, two concepts that are often conflated. Forgiveness is different from reconciliation; forgiveness is one act and reconciliation another. To forgive can be a theological act, or an act motivated by one's religious framework. However, forgiveness can also be psychological and political. To forgive one who has done me harm can occur as a personal, private act without the other knowing, or it can occur with both parties participating.

We will reach a place in our transformational healing, where we are psychologically and spiritually faced with the choice to forgive those who have done us harm. What do we do? How can we possibly forgive those who have caused us such trauma and injury? We choose to forgive, so to release interminable hatred, anger, rage, and resentment from destroying our overall well-being; to refuse such a release means we are choosing to allow pain and injury to continue to disrupt ourselves. We are choosing to allow the perpetrators of our traumas to continue to exercise power over our lives. Unforgiveness keeps us in psycho-emotional and spiritual bondage. Instead, we can consciously choose to exercise compassion and self-love as essential actions in our own transformational healing process. We can free ourselves from further harm in body, mind, spirit, and soul. We can choose to forgive.

To forgive is *not* to forget; nor is it the same as being reconciled. We *must* remember and mourn our soul-wounding. It is a matter of liberating ourselves, and this does not preclude experiencing rage and anger. To forgive those who harmed us, we must necessarily undergo the pain of our anger and rage and grief involved in acknowledging the serious nature of the trespass, violence, or injustice. We do not forget the pain, the rupture, the deep sense of loneliness, and the violation. We do not ignore it either. We move through it and allow it to change us. We choose to forgive to be free from the past and open to new possibilities. We choose to forgive and remember to be unfettered by continued violence. This kind of forgiveness is often done privately without the knowledge or awareness of the one who has harmed us.

However, the sort of forgiveness required when a perpetrator asks the victim for forgiveness necessitates an acknowledgement on the part of the one doing the asking for pardon. A *metánoia* is presumed, a turning away from one's crimes is a fundamental prerequisite, as is the demonstration of the changed behavior. Reconciliation, unlike forgiveness, entails this and more. Reconciliation presumes that the concerned parties mutually participate and seek peaceful relations. Reconciliation has several stages that involve a *metánoia*, or repentance, acknowledgement of one's role, acceptance of one's responsibility, efforts as healing the breaches of trust, concrete changed behaviors, and a coming together to heal and make something relationally new.

The forgiveness which we address here is different from when a perpetrator seeks forgiveness from an individual as they might represent a community symbol. A poignant example of this kind of forgiveness is illustrated in Simon Wiesenthal's "The Sunflower." In the symposium, a dying SS officer imposed upon Mr. Wiesenthal a situation of such unimaginable horror and victimization to which he simply was not in a moral position to address: the SS officer asked Mr. Wiesenthal to forgive him for his evil deeds and those of the collective Nazi regime. How could Mr. Wiesenthal speak for six million Jews, not to mention the three hundred or more specific Jews and the eighty-nine members of his own family, who had perished at the hands of the young Nazi officer?

Transfiguration

Mr. Wiesenthal was put in an intolerable moral position as a living Jew among so many who had suffered and perished, because of the SS officer and the entire killing machinery of which the officer was an active participant. That the officer experienced what appeared to have been a genuine repentance, a *teshuvah*, as far as his acknowledging the insidious evil of his actions in the one massacre he recited is certainly a beginning; however, he also demonstrated a self-serving interior disposition in his insisting that Mr. Wiesenthal remain with him and listen to his gruesome story.

Yet, Mr. Wiesenthal acted with demonstrative mercy and compassion, as he held the hand of the dying officer, even though his instinct was to flee. He stayed, again and again, at the repeated insistence of the Nazi officer. He attentively listened to the tale of terror laden with viscerally painful images and realities. His act of listening, in and of itself, was an act of kindness, mercy, and humility in the spirit of the Prophet Micah. This staying with, this sitting, holding, listening, being present to another is an act of profound humanity and care. It is noble, and yet it was not merited. Through this threshold of returning, we can choose forgiveness as an act of mercy, self-care, and *bearing witness*.

~

Intentional Invitation

What pulls me towards forgiveness? What are the obstacles in choosing forgiveness? Whom do I need to forgive?

Reverent Reflection

> For my freedom, I choose to forgive.
> For my integrity, I choose to remember.
> For my life, I choose to practice self-care.

23
BEARING WITNESS

"When we listen to another with our full presence, we become sacred vessels of another's soul story."
—Ava Dasya Rasa

Bearing witness means to see or know by personal presence or to observe. One of the important aspects of our transformational healing process is to bear witness to ourselves, to our soul-wounding and our transformational soul-mending, or transfiguration. Bearing witness is a way to enter our own life stories, our trauma narratives, with empathy and validation. This bearing witness can be experienced both within a therapeutic relationship, where the therapist bears witness to our story; and it can also be ourselves who bear witness to our own stories, paying close attention to and caring for our wounded selves. Bearing witness can be an active engaging process, or it can be something that unfolds in silence.

Often a trauma survivor feels alone in their suffering. Sometimes a trauma survivor was utterly invalidated in their soul-wounding experience. This is often the case with incest and sexual abuse, intimate partner violence, and medical trauma. When our stories are witnessed, listened to, acknowledged, validated, and affirmed with empathy, something happens inside us. We can breathe a little easier, knowing that what we have carried inside us for so long, is finding space to be what it is—our stripped down, bare bones, naked self in all our vulnerability being received. This threshold of returning gifts us with resilience, as we allow another and ourselves to bear witness to our trauma tales with lovingkindness.

For us to participate in bearing witness means we establish safety and stability—we learn how to regulate our emotions, avoid emotional overwhelm, and feel safe in our bodies. We rebuild trust relationally, discover our inner strengths and resources, and work through pervasive emotions and behaviors, such as: powerlessness, shame, guilt, low self-worth, self-blame, distrust, and repeating our behavioral patterns of re-enacting our traumas. We bear witness to ourselves through our remembering and lamentations.

As trauma survivors, when we move through our lamentations, we learn how to bear witness to the younger versions of ourselves—inner child, teen, and young adult. We might experience the presence of a unitary self, a single self, or of a multitude of selves. Over time, there may be a deepening experience of a multi-faceted whole

Transfiguration

self, or a fusion of the parts of ourselves, an integration that emerges.

A trauma survivors, we learn to reparent ourselves, by offering ourselves the unconditional love and attentive care we needed in our younger versions of ourselves. Only we can offer our younger selves this kind of care, and we do so by internalizing healthy attachment relations that are learned within the therapeutic relationship. To do this, we need to befriend our younger selves, accept them as they are, and welcome them with curiosity and compassion. As trauma survivors, sometimes we find it challenging to simply be with our inner child. Sometimes, we will want to react to the younger versions of ourselves as our primary attachment figures did. Sometimes, we will emotionally neglect our younger self or engage in hyper-criticism. Or, detach and shut down emotionally. If this is our experience, it is an indication that further attention is needed in healing our shame-based identity and attachment wounding.

We discover we can engage in visibly transformative ways with our younger parts, our inner child, when we are feeling safe and regulated, affirmed and validated. Bearing witness involves listening with the ear of our heart, to what our younger selves are holding inside and want to share. What does the pre-verbal infant in us feel in their body? What does the five-year-old child in us want to share? How does the ten-year-old experience themselves? What struggles is the teen in us facing? What are the emotions that these facets of ourselves are holding? What is the source of their beliefs, which often are myths? What kind of presence can we bring to our soul-wounded younger selves? How willing are we to simply be present, hold hands, and listen to these estranged, wounded aspects of ourselves without judgment or criticism?

We can experience our intense emotions and memories and begin to attend to our wounded selves with self-compassion and forgiveness. As we transform our younger selves, attending to their thoughts, emotions, and body sensations—and their strengths and resources, we can let go of all that no longer serves our well-being. Gradually, our soul-wounding transforms as we embrace our whole selves—our transformed, transfigured selves and new identities with genuine self-love. Our wounded inner child and other wounded facets are calling us, searching for us. They beckon us to come and be with, listen to with the ear of our heart, welcome them with our open hearts, and allow them to shapeshift in our transformational soul-mending, or transfiguration. Bearing witness colors our consciences, as we craft new meaning and value in our transfiguring trauma tales.

Transformational healing, transfiguration, takes time and a willingness to wait for layers of self to reveal what needs attending. This, too, is bearing witness to ourselves. To avoid bearing witness to our own selves is to bypass the depths of our embodied interior landscape, where we traverse the subtle yet complex geography of our hearts and touch the numinous terrain of our souls. It is refusing the spiritual invitation to experience *hesed*.

~

Intentional Invitation
What younger facets of myself are calling for my attention? What does my younger self want to share with me? How might I offer a different kind of love to help my younger self heal?

Reverent Reflection
Come to me beloved and tell me your story.
I am here to listen. Your story is like no other.
Your whole body lived experience is yours alone.
Come and tell me your pain. I am here to welcome all of you.
Tell me what your fears are. I am here to shelter you.
Tell me where your heart aches. I am here to comfort.
Tell me where your soul hurts. I am here to soothe.
I am here to let you know you matter.
Come and tell me your secrets.

24

HESED

"Surely goodness and loving kindness shall follow me all the days of my life, and I will dwell in Yahweh's house forever."
—Psalm 23:6

Hesed, חסד,[42] pronounced kheh-sed, is a Hebrew word for love in action and an attitude found in the Hebrew Scriptures 246 times. Sometimes in the Hebrew Scriptures it refers to the interpersonal relationships between humans; however, most times, it points to the relationship between God and humans. *Hesed* is not just any kind of love but a love that encompasses a multitude of attributes: mercy, kindness, compassion, generosity, fierceness, covenantal love, steadfast love, enduring love, or lovingkindness. It is a word that is difficult to translate into one English word. *Hesed* is not an abstract notion of love or mercy. Rather, it is practical in action—our colleague needs vacation days to help her with her cancer treatment; we offer three of ours. Our child is addicted to opiates, and we offer to help them get into an Intensive

Transfiguration

Outpatient Program, or IOP, yet again. Our neighbor is elderly and alone, and we offer to bring them groceries or weed their lawn. A homeless stranger approaches us asking for money, and while we do not give them money, we do bring them a bag of food. These are all acts of lovingkindness, generosity of heart, mercy, and compassion.

In transforming our soul-wounding into soul-mending, or transfiguration, we emerge with a new world view that includes offering lovingkindness to others and ourselves. Trauma survivors are usually quite generous with helping, supporting, forgiving, and loving others. It is in relation to ourselves that we are most challenged to offer *hesed*. Trauma survivors are practiced in self-condemnation and judgment and not at all practiced in extending to themselves exceptional love and mercy which is exactly what is needed. *Hesed* is another threshold of returning—as we begin the journey of offering our neglected selves this gift, we journey into the inescapable transmutation of the totality of our soul-wounding.

Our wounded selves ache for radical kindness that is faithful, enduring, committed, unconditional, generous, steadfast, and merciful—*hesed*. As we heal our younger, wounded versions of ourselves, the various facets of ourselves, we grow in the capacity to offer ourselves compassion and lovingkindness, or *hesed*. *Hesed* involves compassion but is so much more than compassion. It is more akin to unconditional love and extravagant mercy—Divine Empathy. How do we access this kind of Divine Empathy? We begin with blessed silence and *contemplative prayer*, which enable us to connect with something both inside of us and altogether beyond us.

~

Intentional Invitation
There are many passages in the Hebrew scriptures that use the word lovingkindness. Here are two to reflect on:

> How precious is your loving kindness, God!
> The children of men take refuge under the shadow of your wings.
> (Ps. 36:7)

> Answer me, Yahweh, for your loving kindness is good.
> According to the multitude of your tender mercies, turn to me (Ps. 69:16)

Sit down and draw, paint, or sculpt an image of what *hesed* might mean to you after reading this meditation and the above passages.

Reverent Reflection
Beloved I am yours.
You have nothing to fear.
The divine oil of mercy,
burns away your self-judgments

Transfiguration

and invites you to draw from
the well of divine lovingkindness,
compassion, and goodness.
Have no anxiety at all,
but in everything practice gratitude.
Let your heart's deepest longings,
hidden in your soul,
be known to me.
Let the yearnings inside your skin,
hidden in your soul,
be known to me.
In pools of silence and
rivers flowing of gladness,
Beloved, be still.

25
CONTEMPLATIVE PRAYER

*"Contemplative prayer is
wordless resting in the presence of the divine."*
—Ava Dasya Rasa

What is prayer? What comes to your mind? Talking? Asking God for things? Crying out for help? Singing praises of the glory of God? Worship, praise, intercessory, chant, and song are common types of prayer. In classic Christian spirituality the kind of prayer expression where we use reason, will, memory, affectivity, language, images, and affirmation in active engagement to refer to our experience of the divine is called *cataphatic* prayer. This type of prayer has a role to play in our spiritual lives.

Cataphatic prayer evokes awareness of attributes of the divine and often leads to a personal conversion of heart. Cataphatic prayer invites us to enter into a relationship with the divine, wherein we exchange thoughts and feelings. This kind of prayer is uplifting, supportive, nourishing, joyful, and inspiring; it is often expressed in poetry, literature, imagery, hymnody, and music. Examples of this kind of prayer in Christian spirituality include: Taizé, Gregorian Chant, Liturgy of the Hours, and Praise and Worship.[43] Though cataphatic prayer is aesthetically beautiful and spiritually uplifting, it is primarily a prayer of conversation.

The kind of prayer we need to cultivate our attention, however, is rooted in the art of awareness and surrendering. It is contemplative prayer, where we experience the deeper transformation of our soul-wounds. This kind of prayer requires our listening and noticing. It is a prayer of silence and stillness. It is a prayer that involves opening our whole selves—heart, mind, body, and soul. It involves both witnessing ourselves and self-emptying, or *kenosis*—the self-emptying of all that distracts our attention from both our most authentic selves and the loving presence of the divine. This kind of contemplative prayer is known as *apophatic* prayer, the prayer of negation, or the *via negativa*—no image, sacred nothingness, wordlessness, silence, and darkness.[44]

It is a prayer path to union with the divine: there is nothing but our longing for the divine or sacred, the transcendent, the Invisible, Mystery, the Beloved; and the longing of the divine or sacred, the transcendent, the Invisible, Mystery, the Beloved for us—the creaturely beloved. It is a contemplative path to divine intimacy with the immanent-transcendent experienced in our embodied, incarnate selves. Contemplative prayer opens us up to the potential of full receptivity through total surrender. This kind of prayer is a threshold to returning through which we pass to rest wordless in the loving presence of the divine, the Heart of God. As we go deeper into silence, and enter the creative sacred energies buried in the numinous terrain of our soul, our embodied being, we encounter Mystery—and meeting Mystery changes us. One method of cultivating this kind of contemplative prayer is known as Centering Prayer.

Centering Prayer

Centering Prayer is a path to transformation and transcendence of self. It is a way to cultivate our abiding in the presence of the Divine. Centering Prayer involves our intentionality: our spiritual consciousness, awareness, and willingness to surrender our false selves and all that distracts us from becoming our authentic selves. When we begin Centering Prayer, soon after we become practiced in experiencing a quieting of our interior life, sometimes only a few months into this spiritual practice, unconscious aspects of our soul-wounding will surface into our wakeful consciousness, and this will likely be painful. It is painful to awaken to our distressing, wounded, fragmented selves.

Our fears, disappointments, anger, shame, and overall sense of woundedness are revealed. This is jarring at first. We do not want to face these wounded aspects of ourselves; yet, unless we sit with these facets, we will remain stuck in our fragmented selves. To engage in Centering Prayer, we do need to have the capacity to sustain our ventral vagal state for some period of time. We do need to be able to hold space for our distress with compassionate curiosity. Once we begin our Centering Prayer practice, we will grow our distress tolerance muscles, so that, over time, we will no longer resist meeting our soul-wounded selves.

Our false, maladaptive, performative self—our shame-based persona that is imbued with a sense of separateness from the divine, others, and creation, transforms deeply through a radical surrendering and *kenosis*, or the self-emptying process. We must be patient, as this is an unfolding process that cannot be forced. It is a gradual, slow transformational process. There will be times when we are uncomfortable, and we will need *to be with* our distress. There is no spiritual bypassing in the journey of soul-wounding to soul-mending, or transfiguration.

In Centering Prayer through the use of breath, sacred word, or image, we are at once deeply stilled as if asleep and yet acutely present:

> I was asleep, but my heart was awake.
> It is the voice of my beloved who knocks.
> (Song of Sol. 5:2)

These words from the exquisite and erotically charged scripture song-poem, *Song of Songs* (Fourth poem), point to what Centering Prayer is about. "I sleep"—when we begin to experience Centering Prayer, which is a renewed form of an ancient prayer path leading into deeper or pure contemplation, we quiet our minds, our bodies, our spirits. "But my heart is awake!" Yes. Our hearts are awake, alert, watchful, waiting, attending, and opening to the presence of the Beloved, the Divine Heart, or Divine Indwelling. For Christians, this is the Christ, or Mother-Father God, the Trinity, or the Spirit Holy. It is Mystery. The Invisible. The Wordless, The Unsayable. The Beloved.[45]

In our embodied being we abide in the loving presence of the divine; we breathe the breath of the divine. We discover a pool of blessed stillness at our depths, as we move about in our ordinary wakefulness. We bring into blessed stillness all the concepts, images, and words we carry within us and those which assault our senses daily in the marketplace. We empty ourselves of all that we carry inside our wounded skin—our untrue selves, false egos, attachments to our thoughts, masks we construct for the public, fears, guilt, shame, and wounds, including our perceived separateness from the divine.

We become open and receptive to meeting ourselves in our soul-wounding.[46] In our self-emptying we surrender all that impedes our most authentic selves, we befriend the wounded aspects of ourselves, and in doing so, we become aware of the divine energies lying beneath the numinous terrain our soul, our embodied being. Our false selves morph or transform into our more authentic selves, especially as we bear witness to our soul-wounds. We offer the gift of hospitality with *hesed* to our wounded selves as we become more vulnerable.

Eventually, over time, with practice, we will come to the still point within, where we are simply resting in the presence of our Beloved, pure Infinite Love. With time, we wake up to the experience of encountering our authentic selves revealing our unveiled faces; this awareness infuses our senses—seeing, hearing, touching, smelling, tasting. We are alive in our embodied knowing and unknowing—the dialectic of recognizing the loving Presence of the divine within, while also recognizing we are met with infinite Mystery in all of creation. This divine loving Presence is beyond all words, concepts, and ideas. We come into this Presence in our breath, our blood, our flesh, our thoughts, emotions, body sensations, our embodied yearning—our soul.

We cease all our doing to simply *be* in the loving Presence within, the Divine Indwelling. "With my soul I have desired you in the night. Yes, with my spirit within me I will seek you earnestly;"(Isa. 26:9). Through the practice of growing awareness, waiting, and surrendering in Centering Prayer, over time, we arrive at a place of transformative grace: awakened consciousness, interior quiet, stillness, and receptivity to the Divine Indwelling, or Heart of God. Centering Prayer cultivates pure contemplation. In pure contemplation, our hearts are cracked open; we are naked before the Divine. Centering Prayer, then, is a threshold of returning, where we enter into our transfiguration and divine intimacy, and we become fully conscious that we are not separate from the Source of our breath, others, and the whole of creation. And, it is here, in this intimate encounter with the Heart of the Divine that we are bathed in *the oil of mercy*!

~

Intentional Invitation
"Be still, and know that I am God" (Ps. 46:10). Set aside 20 minutes daily to still your body, pay attention with your whole being, listen deeply with the ear of your heart and practice Centering Prayer.[47]

Reverent Reflection
We abandon all that we are—our waking selves, our sleeping selves, our false selves, our ego-centered selfishness, our wondrous selves. Through radical grace, we freely surrender our whole selves in all that we are in our human condition—the light, the shadow, and everything messy in between. We sink into our center, deep into the sacred dwelling place, where, in silence, we are stripped bare before inexhaustible Mystery.

26
OIL OF MERCY

"I will also give you a new heart, and I will put a new spirit within you. I will take away the stony heart out of your flesh, and I will give you a heart of flesh."
—Ezekiel 36:26

When we anoint our deepest wounds and fragmented selves with the oil of mercy—the loving presence of a compassionate, accepting, tender, and empathic self, our bearing witness self, we experience a radical transformation of our hearts of stone into hearts of flesh. Our hearts of stone were fossilized with imprints of our lived traumas: physical abuse—beatings with a belt, emotional and verbal abuse—condescending words and tone demeaning us, a critical, punitive raging adult reminding us, again and again, how we are unworthy, a mistake, a problem, stupid, ugly, someone to neglect, abuse, bully, diminish, or abandon. Sexual traumas—sexual harassment, molestation, incest, and rape. Or psychological trauma—the oppressive expectation of us neither having nor expressing any distressing emotions and expecting us to be perfect. Or, having had parents with mental illness, parents who neglected us altogether or parents who parentified us (expected children to act as parents taking care of siblings and parents).

These and so many more traumas, such as: microaggressions about race, ethnicity, sexual orientation, gender identity, or able-bodiedness are impressed on our hearts of stone. Our hearts of stone felt impenetrable. As if they encased the ink dark black of our childhood, the terror of adolescence, and the self-blame and deep, debilitating shame of our adulthood. Our hearts of stone protected us. Kept us alive against the odds. They are the rock out of which the tomb that kept us hidden and isolated in the dark is hewn. They are also the rock out of which our visceral longing for the possibility of a different, renewed life of connection is hewn.

The oil of mercy washes over us, bathes us in a liberation we could not have imagined. Mercy is upon us, despite our wounded souls, our fear-filled lives, our shame-based identities, our inability to heal. Mercy pours over our imperfections that have held us in a bondage for years and it releases these flaws from judgment. Mercy is what it is precisely because we have done nothing, absolutely nothing to merit such extravagant kindness. We receive this offering humbly. The oil of mercy becomes the anointing oil of our gratitude, as we pass through this threshold of returning. Behold the beauty of our authentic selves still unfolding, ever

Transfiguration

ancient, ever new. We now know that with hearts of flesh we have been bathed in the oil of mercy and are *transfigured*.

~

Intentional Invitation

Make a visual collage image of your heart of stone and your heart of flesh. Once your collage is completed, place it on an altar and bless it with a ceremony, burning sage or sweet grass.

Reverent Reflection

Mother
Morning Star,
sees, hears, bears
ten thousand,
white-hot mercies.
Behold

27
TRANSFIGURATION

"Transfiguration is the journey of plumbing the depths of our embodied interior landscape, traversing the subtle yet complex geography of our hearts and touching the numinous terrain of our souls."
—Ava Dasya Rasa

Transfiguration breathes a new spirit in us, a renewed life and spirituality: we have been resuscitated from our barely surviving, gasping selves and are reconciled with our wounded, fragmented selves and able to breathe deeply. A new life arises out of the transfiguring of our soul-wound. Paradoxically, as we experience a loss of clear-cut answers we emerge with a new strength of resilience in vulnerability. We are connected to our authentic selves and the whole of creation, as if we are awakening to discover the impressive wonder of the vast cosmos.

We begin to know ourselves from the depth of our embodied interior landscape, once desolate, bare desert now lush with berries and blooms, vibrant and welcoming. Our hearts of flesh remind us of our path of transformational healing, the transfiguration of the beauty and terror of our magnificent lives. From the pulse of our hearts of flesh, we now embrace our wise self, standing on holy ground, where we welcome all aspects of ourselves: grief and sorrow, despair and fear, hope and heartaches, immense stillness and silence, wonder and awe, and gratitude and joy. We recognize our authentic selves and glimpse the divine in all our embodied humanity and in all of creation.

Our transfiguration awakens our soul, opening to the Way of Love that embraces our whole lived lives with unconditional acceptance and affirmation. Our souls, once mute, as we bent low *crushed in spirit* under the oppression of our *bread of affliction*, reawaken. Transfiguration gifts us with our soul's voice once again—we speak our trauma tales in truth and grace. We now know we have been fired in the furnace of Infinite Love. We have been walking through the thresholds of returning that have become our spiritual path to our authentic, transfigured selves.

We encountered our *ruptures* and *crises*, as we *embarked* in *safety* though in *darkness*. We *surrendered* and learned to *wait* and *lament* and *befriend*. E*nfleshed* we have *emptied* ourselves of all that distracts and depletes our deepest longings and embodied spirit selves. We have practiced *holy listening* with the ear of our heart in our *desert wilderness*.

We have learned *self-compassion* as we stilled ourselves in *silence* and *solitude*. We are *bearers of witness* to our life stories, and our renewed narratives write us forward into empowerment and connectivity. We are learning to *forgive* and practice *hesed* towards ourselves, as we center ourselves down in *contemplative prayer* into the depth of the mystery of our lives. Bathed in the *oil of mercy,* our faltering soul fragments are redeemed, made anew as a cohesive, integrative whole infused and illuminated with the *kintsugi* gold of our transfiguration.

We have come home in full *presence* to our transformed, *transfiguring* selves—a place of belonging. We now know we are incarnationally interdependent on the whole of creation. We belong in the community of the cosmos. In our heart's deepest longings for connection with something altogether beyond our earthen vessels, we come into the loving presence of the Divine Indwelling and come to understand the Beloved is within us—and that we, too, are the beloved. We are transfigured and we are ready to *begin again*.

~

Intentional Invitation

Reflect on your transformational healing journey thus far: where are you noticing transfiguration unfolding? Choose an object to symbolize your transfiguring process and place it on an altar with a recent photo of yourself. What about the object speaks to your transformation? Write down an affirmation that speaks to your transfiguration.

Reverent Reflection

heart of my heart
soul of my soul
breath that breathes
me into life.
wound of my wound
your morning fragrance—
cedar in the desert
perfumes my whole body.
heart of my heart,
wound of my wound
you have sought me
from the wild waters
of the stony shores,
over the mountains
into dry land.
living flame,
fire of my soul
you lured me
into your
secret chamber—
breathless
I am transfigured!

28

BEGIN AGAIN

"She wants to become those two wild geese, that with beating wings rise high aloft."
—Anonymous
From "Nineteen Old Poems"

To begin again is to say "yes," wholeheartedly to the promise of infinite possibilities that is revealed moment to moment, as we emerge from our transformational healing from soul-wounding to soul-mending, or transfiguration. It is a threshold moment before returning. Returning to where? To ourselves—a place of belonging. Our most authentic selves, transformed from ego-centric, false, maladaptive, performative, shame-based selves to revealed, transmuted, transformed, divine-centered, authentic selves—the true, wholly imperfect, most accepting version of ourselves rooted in the numinous terrain of our soul, our embodied being. We begin again from a radically different vantage point: we are profoundly changed, so that we are responding rather than reacting to life's circumstances, invitations, and challenges.

Transfiguration

We participate in life with intentionality rather than act as its powerless victims. Transformational healing of our soul-wounds is not a linear process; rather, it involves moving forward and back and sometimes to the side then down and up in a spiral dance. It is multi-layered and fluid, rather than one dimensional and static. Sometimes it might feel like parts of us are dying when we are undergoing the fire of transformative healing that calls us to begin again. This is because we are dying to false self as we experience self-transcendence. We are changed through our transformational healing—neuro-biologically, psycho-emotionally, physically, and spiritually—we are transfigured.

I think of the story of Lazarus in the Gospel of John 11: 1-44, where Jesus performs one of the most well-known and impressive miracles of his ministry on earth. He calls Lazarus out of his entombment where he lay dead for four days. Early in the story we learn that Jesus is told "the one you love is sick" (John 11:3). We know that Jesus loved Lazarus and his sisters, Martha and Mary. Yet when Jesus learned about Lazarus falling ill, he chose to remain where he was for two more days and then he returned to Judea to see Lazarus who had already died.

When Jesus arrived in Bethany, he learned that Lazarus had been in the tomb for four days. Martha went out to meet Jesus at the gate (not in her home but at the distant gate), and in genuine emotional honesty confronted him; "if you had been here, my brother would not have died" (John 11:21). Then Martha affirmed her belief, "God will give you whatever you ask" (John 11:22) to which Jesus replied, "Your brother will rise again" (John 11:23). Martha failed to grasp the full theological meaning of this statement and seemed to think Jesus was referring to the "resurrection in the last day" (John 11: 24).

Jesus responded by saying, "I am the resurrection and the life. The one who believes in me will live, even though they die, and whoever lives by believing in me will never die. Do you believe this?" (John 11: 25-26). Martha reaffirmed her belief and then called her sister Mary, who ran to Jesus, fell to her knees, and cried, "Lord, if you had been here, my brother would not have died" (John 11:32). When Jesus saw her weeping, he, too, wept. He was deeply moved and as he came to the tomb he directed the others there, "Take away the stone" (John 11:39). Martha in her usual forthright personality and temperament reminded Jesus that there will be a "bad odor," since her brother had been in the tomb for four days. Jesus prayed, and he then called Lazarus out from the tomb, "Lazarus, come out" (John 11:43). The gospel states, the dead man came out, his hands and feet wrapped with strips of linen, and a cloth around his face. Jesus said to them, "Take off the grave clothes and let him go" (John 11: 44).

Transfiguration

I wonder why Jesus didn't go to the sickbed of Lazarus before he died. Why did he intentionally wait two additional days before going to see the one he loved? Trauma survivors often wonder, too, why human and divine help doesn't show up sooner before we are subjected to even more soul-wounding? Why must we suffer at all?! Why must our healing take so long, for what seems like an eternity? Are we not deserving of human and divine help now?! Where is our miracle?! I do not presume to have the answers to such legitimate psychological and theological questions.

Here is what I do know: Jesus wept with Mary and for Lazarus—and he weeps with us. The Divine weeps with us. Higher Power weeps with us. The Loving One weeps with us. The Compassionate One weeps with us. God weeps with us. Spirit weeps with us. The Beloved weeps with us. We are not spared existential sufferings even those that are unspeakable. We can and will suffer. Not all people suffer in the same way. But certainly, all people suffer in many different ways.

We are soul-wounded, and we each have a Lazarus in us. Lazarus has its roots in the Hebrew name רזעלא, Elʿāzār (Eleazar),[48] which means "the one who God has helped." How we attend our trauma wounds will determine if our wounding becomes the stuff of our trust, our faith, which propels us forward into a life worth living; or, if it will lead us to succumb to a life that is dead and rotting from the stench of fear and doubt.

What will we do with our disappointments, losses, and all the things we cannot control? If we choose to keep our most authentic selves at the gate, at a distance, we also keep our experience of the Infinite, Mystery, or Unsayable at the distant gate.

Transformative healing means we own our rage, our moral outrage, our fury at the violations, injustices, trespasses, insanities, and inhumanities that have been inscribed on our souls and in our bodies and minds and hearts. We need to weep from the deep well of our grief. We must enter our wound in the tomb of our darkness. We cannot escape our need to own our wounded histories, move through them with safety therapeutically, both neuro-biologically and relationally, befriend them, attend them with compassionate empathy, and then surrender them through *kenosis* into the fire of our transformation, which transfigures us.

Our miracle comes when we undertake the hard work of our inner transformational healing that leads us to our transfiguration. Our transfiguration will not necessarily answer our most acute theological questions of God and existential questions of suffering; nor will it necessarily soothe our disruptive psychological understandings. Our transfiguration will reveal, however, what is possible despite our deepest wounding—our unspeakable violations, abuses, and torments. We encounter the Infinite, Mystery, and Unsayable in our transfiguring from false selves to authentic selves. We can

Transfiguration

and do begin again in our newfound identities and in our revised narratives. We come to bear witness to the reality that Divine Empathy is present in our psychological, emotional, and spiritual desert and desolation, as well as in our moments of flourishing with bountiful blooms and berries.

The tomb of Lazarus had a stench after four days and yet Jesus approached the tomb and asked that the rock be rolled away to be with that which others would find offensive or intolerable. Here is the paradox of transforming trauma and spirituality: amid the stench of our wound, the place of our total pain, the tomb of our wounding draws the fragrance of Divine Empathy, unbounded *hesed*, Pure Love—the Invisible, Mystery, and Unsayable. Divine Empathy whispers: I am with you in your pain. The mess of your life. In your distress. In your disappointment. In your abandonment. In your violation. In your rage. In your hurt. In your fear. In your confusion. In your addiction. In your trauma. In your shame. In your loneliness. In your self-loathing. In your weeping. The Infinite, the Beloved, weeps with us in our broken heartedness, desperation, loss, sickness, poverty, shame, frustration, fear, rage, and hopelessness.

Divine Empathy opens us up to the possibility that we can be raised up to new life even after all that we have been through—be it four days, four years, or forty years in our tombs. The dead place in us, our Lazarus, comes out into the light, as the stone is rolled away, and our dry bones live (Ezek. 37:1-6). Dead comes to life! We begin again! What is called forth in us is not the old self that is wounded and dead, but the transformed self now transfigured and alive. The new self is deeply connected to all that matters from the inside out—all that is real and true and good and beautiful and distressing and awful and horrifying, and all of it is rooted in both darkness and loss and light and life. The tomb of our heart is rolled away to reveal the womb of our soul, which gives birth to our *authenticity*.

~

Intentional Invitation

What is hidden behind the tomb of your heart? Journal your answer. Sit with your words. Ponder them. See what emerges in images and emotions and body sensations. Breathe. Now breathe again.

Reverent Reflection

Take off your "grave clothes" and pray:

May I begin again with fresh eyes and attend to what is newly rising in me.

May I begin again with a humble heart to attend to what has always been rising in me.

May I begin again with a hopeful spirit to attend to what may still yet arise in me.

29
AUTHENTICITY

"Am I then yet unwilling to go about that, for which I myself was born and brought forth into this world?"
—Marcus Aurelius

When we feel at home in our own skin, have made peace with our human imperfections, and are aligned with our soul's purpose, we have come home to our authentic selves—and we finally belong. Our authentic selves are real: we acknowledge we bleed and break at times; we accept our limitations and liabilities. We accept the inherent sorrow and grief in our human condition. We acknowledge our heart's longing for something altogether transcendent. We affirm our ability to transform and change and grow into all that we are meant to be. We strive to become the absolute best versions of ourselves given our station in life. Authentic living is soulful living, and it means we no longer merely survive; rather, we thrive! We choose to flourish!

We have a sense of Spirit in the here and now and experience something of the Mystery of the Transcendent. Our intuitive senses are heightened, and our wise-minded skills are honed. We realize our insides match our outsides and we are free. We no longer perform ourselves wearing masks for the world. We step into our own life scripts that we have revised and show ourselves to the world with openness and vulnerability of heart. We welcome new opportunities, and we identify new life missions. We are more attuned to our needs as well as the needs of others. When we do give, it is from our plenty and not from our insecurities, a need to please, or fear of rejection. We know we can survive the worst and thrive with the best. We belong.

Where we were once helpless and alone, disconnected from others and ourselves, we become empowered and connected to ourselves and others. We live seamlessly rather than in soul fragments. Our sense of self is coherent, functional, and integrated. We hold space for ourselves from a place of self-love and self-respect. Our sufferings of self-loathing and self-disgust are a faint memory. The neurobiological and emotional activations we once suffered intensely are transformed into the ability to live life most of the time from our social engagement, or ventral vagal complex. In our embodied regulated self, we now *know*—we engage the world with an integrated awareness and consciousness through our lived experiential embodied encounters.

Transfiguration

We step into our self-understanding having undergone a transformation from the inside out. We experienced a lived account of our trauma. This is not an intellectual or reflective analytical analysis; rather, it is our direct granular experiences of human suffering that have been palpably transformed. We perceive life from a point of connectivity and creativity and courage. Our life is a blend of light and dark, brightness and shadows, contours and contrasts, depth and surface, all things and nothingness—a chiaroscuro tapestry of our transfigured embodied soul. We meet our authentic selves as we are transfigured by Divine Empathy. And we are in *awe*!

~

Intentional Invitation
Write your life's mission statement: to what do you feel called? What is your life purpose? What are your core values and beliefs considering your transformational healing of trauma and spirituality? Your transfiguration? What do you want to leave as your legacy?

Reverent Reflection
>In the dark waning of crescent moon
>night wounds my sleep.
>No longer is my pillow stone—
>I rise to silent music sounding
>from all the tabernacles in the world!

30
AWE

"In your body is the garden of flowers. Take your seat on the thousand petals of the lotus, and there gaze on the Infinite Beauty."
—Kabir

Transfiguring, we have passed through many thresholds to return to our most authentic selves always already rooted in the numinous terrain of our souls, our embodied being. Here we enter a deeper vulnerability that allows us to step into soulful living. We awaken to experience a sense of awe. Wonder. Amazement. Reverence. Astonishment—awe embraces us, gratitude humbles us, and joy infuses us.

We experience life as it truly is, a dialectic: suffused with unspeakable sufferings, human failings, distressing natural disasters, depth of grief and sorrow, and unimaginable heartbreaks; and it is a wondrous creation filled with miracles, kindness, beauty, magic, creativity, intelligences, mystery, and wonders beyond wonders!

Transfiguration

This is awe: that in the midst of the inescapable human horrors, we also experience moments of brave heroism, inexplicable kindness, generosity of heart, hope-filled acts of love, empathy, forgiveness, service, redemption—and Infinite Beauty!

When we are transfiguring, we reach a place in our transformational healing journey where we can sustain social engagement in our ventral vagal state—we are calm, connected, present, communicative, empathic, curious, creative, courageous, open and receptive. While we are not in our ventral vagal state at all times, we do learn how to navigate moving in and out of our ventral vagal, sympathetic, and dorsal vagal states. This ability to self-regulate allows us to experience life at a radically different level.

When we experience awe, we are in a state neurobiologically that mirrors the state we are in during contemplative prayer—we are grounded, rooted, stilled and silenced. We experience equanimity. We are receptive. In this state, awe wraps itself around us. We are often left breathless and feeling small in the face of the enormity of the palpable wonderment of all creation and the cosmos. Yet, awe also empowers and emboldens us as human beings who are capable of imagining, creating, exploring, and loving.

Awe is the mother of gratitude and joy. When we experience awe, our gratitude practice grows, which, in turn, gives birth to open-hearted joy. Transfiguration's trinity of awe, gratitude, and joy are intimately interconnected. Awe gives birth to gratitude which humbles us; the practice of gratitude nurtures the soil from which our joy blossoms. This dynamic trio affirms our life and gives it both immanent and transcendent meaning. This awe-gratitude-joy trinity can be quiet or exalted.

We feel awe in our whole mind, body, spirit, and soul, as we walk through created nature—a cathedral of aspens resplendent and shimmering golden in the October sun. We feel awe when we are stopped in our tracks in the hushed hours on a cold winter's dawn—skies announcing a veritable watercolor of brilliant pinks and deep purples bleeding to the edges of infinity. We feel gratitude tasting the first sip of a piping hot bowl of minestrone soup, after trudging home in a bitter freezing snowstorm. We recognize joy that comes with the unannounced brush of our lover's hand, signaling another fiery beginning in our blood and bones. Awe flourishes beneath the skin of our gratitude and joy.

Transfiguration gifts us with grace that enlarges our capacity for "being there," being fully present in this moment to experience awe in the ordinary and extraordinary moments of our lives—a sunrise announcing hope for the new day, a birdsong quieting our spirit, the gentle touch of a loved one's hand in ours, the astounding view from a mountaintop, ocean

Transfiguration

waves rising, cresting, and crashing onto the shore, watching the first landing of humankind on the moon, listening to a young inaugural poet speak words that inspire and awaken, our sense of family and belonging, and the solemnity and respect with which we honor our fallen ones.

Remembering moments of awe inspires our practice of gratitude and it cultivates our humility, which nurtures our receptivity to welcome genuine joy. Joy transcends happiness in that we can experience moments of unimagined joy during moments of tremendous suffering—a new mother wails in labor, while experiencing indescribable joy at the first glimpse of her newborn. The Hebrew word for remember is "zakar,"[49] and one of its meanings is "being there." We remember that being there—present, open, connected, and vulnerable with our authentic selves and all of life is how we participate in the incomprehensible awe in life. Awe connects us with the ineffable Mystery of life that is manifested in our embodied selves and throughout the whole of creation and beyond all universes.

Exuberant grace ignites pure awe. Out of the depths of our fully present incarnational connection to our human and divine heart, we are grateful that we experience unexpected moments of awe. Awe burns away our fear, and, with gratitude, accompanies us into a joy that is set afire inside our most tender hearts. Awe arises viscerally as we breathe deeply from our transfigured authentic selves, which are rooted in the numinous terrain of our soul, our embodied being. Do we dare undergo the transformative journey of transfiguration that gives us the gift of awe? Do we dare enter the mystery of our transfigured lives with reverent awe? Do we dare burn with the fire of human-divine joy? Do we dare surrender our sleeping, soul-wounded fragmented selves for hearts awakened, as soul-mended, transformed, transfigured beloveds, drenched in Love's Infinite delight?[50]

~

Intentional Invitation

What does *awe* mean for you? What does *awe-gratitude-joy* mean for you? Can you think of a time when you experienced genuine awe? Where were you? What emotions arose? What thoughts did you have? What sensations did you feel in your body? Write it. Color it. Paint it. Draw it. Sculpt it. Compose it. Dance it. Sing it. Be with it. Celebrate it!

Reverent Reflection

> Beloved quench—
> drink deeply
> my sweet nectar

EPILOGUE

"I shall make well all that is not well."
—Julian of Norwich

A Prayer for Transfiguration

O Compassionate One, you have gathered us here in-between ink and page on this dark night of our journey, as a people in search of transforming our trauma and spirituality:

May we welcome our transfigured lives unfolding in safety, stability, healing, and wholeness.
May the Spirit Holy illumine us to open our eyes to see, our ears to hear, and our hearts to receive and embrace ourselves in all our blessed wounded imperfection.
May we seek to be safe.
May we seek to be of sound mind.
May we seek the courage to transform.
May we seek to know ourselves as we continue becoming all that is possible.

May we know we are infinitely loved, as we learn to love ourselves and others.
May our lives be touched with moments of awe.
May we practice gratitude each moment.
May our joy be a light to others.
May we embrace ourselves as we surrender to an ongoing transfiguring process.
May our transfigured lives be a living sacrament for our bruised and broken world.
May we meet the Beloved always present within our soul.
And may the words of our mouths and the meditations of our hearts be affirming and life-giving.
May it be so.

APPENDIX A

Centering Prayer Guidelines[51]

The following brief guidelines for Centering Prayer are an adaptation based on the work of Thomas Keating, OSCO:

1. Choose a *sacred* word or short phrase, such as: Peace, Trust, Let Go, Calm, Breathe, Mercy, Listen, Love, Hesed, or Receive. This word symbolizes your openness to be present to the divine.

2. As you quiet yourself sitting in a noble and dignified position, close your eyes or lower your gaze.

3. Breathe from your diaphragm and still your whole body.

4. As you notice your thoughts arise, gently use your sacred word to focus your attention, as you let your

thoughts rise and fall; or you may elect to focus on your breath. Thoughts can include: cognitions, feelings, sensations, images, or memories.

5. At the end of your meditation period, usually 20 minutes, stay in place quiet for a few minutes to simply be with yourself in the silence of the moment.

NOTES

1. My understanding of transfiguration is informed by both the neurobiology of trauma and Christian mystics, especially the spirituality and teaching of Meister Eckhart. See: Maurice O'C Walshe, trans., *The Complete Works of Meister Eckhart,* (New York: Herder & Herder, 2009).

2. "Divine Empathy" is a phrase I coined to describe the kind of empathy that extends beyond our ordinary everyday experiences of empathy. What distinguishes this kind of empathy is its extraordinary generosity and unconditional commitment to enter into presence and relationship with another who is in need of our empathy. We experience Divine Empathy both through our human relations and in our transcendent experiences of the divine.

3. "Fragmented parts of ourselves" and "wounded, fragmented selves:" I use these phrases throughout the book. They refer to both our fragmented parts, resulting from dissociation that we may experience from our trauma and the disintegrated parts of ourselves that need transformation, so as to be reintegrated into a "whole" self that may or may not be a unitary self. Our fragmentation is both a trauma wounding and a source of our trauma resilience.

4. "Thresholds of returning" is a phrase I coined to describe the sacred gateways or portals through which we are called to pass, as we transform our soul-wounds to soul-mending, or transfiguration. As we undergo a transfiguring process, we return to our authentic selves, hidden yet always already rooted in the numinous terrain of our soul, our embodied being.

5. "What is Trauma?" Big Think, accessed December 30, 2022, 2:58. https://www.youtube.com/watch?v=BJfmfkDQb14

6. The term "container" is a term used in the context of psychotherapy. It refers to a therapeutic holding space or environment. It is also used in Eye Movement Desensitization & Reprocessing, or EMDR, as a resourcing tool.

7. The fawn response, coined by psychotherapist Peter Walker, licensed Marriage and Family psychotherapist, describes (often unconscious) behavior that aims to please, appease, and neutralize the threat to keep ourselves safe from further harm. Pete Walker, MA, MFT, "Codependency, Trauma, and the Fawn Response," *The East Bay Therapist*, (Jan/Feb, 2003): 1. http://www.pete-walker.com/codependencyFawnResponse.htm.

8. Judith Lewis Herman, *Trauma & Recovery: The Aftermath of Violence from Domestic Abuse to Political Terror* (Basic Books, 1992), 155.

9. Herman, *Trauma & Recovery*, 175.

10. To learn about the neuroscience model of the "window of tolerance," as coined by Dan Siegal, Clinical Professor of Psychiatry, see: "How To Help Your Clients Understand the Window of Tolerance," National Institute for the Clinical Application of Behavioral Medicine, accessed September 6, 2022, https://www.nicabm.com/trauma-how-to-help-your-clients-understand-their-window-of-tolerance/

11. The fawn, or "please and appease" response is common with narcissistic partners or caregivers in abusive relationships. Stephen W. Porges, PhD, author of the *Polyvagal Theory: Neurophysiological Foundations of Emotions, Attachment, Communication, and Self-Regulation* (Norton, 2011), Distinguished University Scientist, Professor of Psychiatry, and Founder Director of the Traumatic Stress Research Consortium, offers an insightful explication of the please and appease, or fawn response. See: NICABM, "Treating Trauma: When Working with Please and Appease," YouTube video, December 15, 2022, 1:35, https://www.youtube.com/watch?v=9mPNvFQTVa0.

12. Stephen W. Porges, PhD, "Experts," NICABM, accessed December 18, 2022, https://www.nicabm.com/experts/stephen-porges/

13. NICABM, "How the Nervous System Responds to Trauma," accessed December 18, 2022, https://www.nicabm.com/topic/trauma-responses/

14. Deb Dana, *The Polyvagal Theory in Therapy*, read by Coleen Marlo, (Old Saybrook: Tantor Media, 2019), Audible, 3:11.

15. Dana, *The Polyvagal Theory in Therapy*, 3:36.

16. Stephen W. Porges, PhD, "Experts," NICABM, accessed December 18, 2022, https://www.nicabm.com/experts/stephen-porges/

17. Dana, 4:03.

18. Ibid. 6:15.

19. Carl R. Rogers, "A Theory of Therapy, Personality, and Interpersonal Relationships: As Developed in the Client-Centered Framework," in *Psychology: A study of a science, Vol. 3*,

Formulations of the person and the social context, ed. S. Koch (New York: McGraw Hill, 1959), 184-256. Carl R. Rogers believed listening deeply to a client without judgment is having unconditional positive regard, or unconditional acceptance; according to Rogers, providing unconditional regard allows clients to attain self-actualization (Maslow's hierarchy of needs) through their own internal resources.

20. Rhona Lewis, "Erikson's 8 Stages of Psychosocial Development, Explained for Parents," Healthline, April 28, 2020. https://www.healthline.com/health/parenting/erikson-stages

21. Such trauma therapies include: Brainspotting, EMDR, Somatic Experiencing,™ Somatic Attachment, Trauma-Sensitive Mindfulness, Sensorimotor Therapy, Neuro-Affective Relational Model (NARM), and Internal Family Systems (IFS). Supportive adjunct therapies include Grief Recovery, Depth Psychotherapy, Dialectical Behavior Therapy (DBT), Sand Tray, Creative Expression/Art Therapy, Acceptance and Commitment Therapy (ACT), and Contemplative Spirituality & Renewal.

22. See: https://www.stephenporges.com/ for the groundbreaking work of Stephen W. Porges, PhD on the polyvagal theory and for more details related to the autonomic nervous system's role in emotions and trauma responses.

23. Dana, *The Polyvagal Theory in Therapy,* 4:40. For an in-depth analysis of the study of the role of neuroception in safety, see: Stephen W. Porges, PhD, "Polyvagal Theory: A Science of Safety," *Front Integr. Neurosci.,* 10 May 2022: 2, https://doi.org/10.3389/fnint.2022.871227

24. Box breathing uses diaphragmatic breathing. Rest one hand on your belly and the other on your chest. Inhale through your nose counting 4 seconds, holding at the top of the breath 4

seconds, exhaling while blowing out through your mouth 4 seconds, and resting 4 seconds.

25. K. Gallagher, "The Bread of Affliction," GraceinTorah, April 17, 2019. https://graceintorah.net/2019/04/17/the-bread-of-affliction/

26. Rabbi Danielle Upbin, "Ha Lachma Anya: The Bread of Slavery and Affliction," My Jewish Learning. https://www.myjewishlearning.com/article/ha-lachma-anya-the-bread-of-slavery-and-affliction/

27. H3820, Hebrew Dictionary (Lexicon Concordance), accessed January 7, 2023. http://lexiconcordance.com/hebrew/3820.html

28. See meditation number 25, Contemplative Prayer, for more in depth discussion of Centering Prayer.

29. Rudolf Otto, *The Idea of the Holy* (Oxford University Press, London/New York/Toronto/Ontario, 1923), 12.

30. Benedict, Saint, Abbot of Monte Cassino, prologue to *The Rule of St. Benedict*, ed. Timothy Fry, OSB (Collegeville: Liturgical Press, 1982), 15.

31. Benedict, Saint, Abbot of Monte Cassino, prologue, 15.

32. Simone Weil, *Gravity & Grace* (New York: Routledge, 2002), 117.

33 William Johnston, *The Still Point: Reflections on Zen and Christian Mysticism* (New York: 1970).

34. Kintsugi Spirit, "What Is Kintsugi? Discover its history, its technique and its symbol," accessed December 31, 2022,

https://esprit-kintsugi.com/en/quest-ce-que-le-kintsugi/#:~:text=The%20word%20Kintsugi%20comes%20from,several%20weeks%20or%20even%20months.

35. Robyn Griggs Lawrence, "Wabi-Sabi: The Art of Imperfection," *Utne Reader,* October 27, 2007, https://www.utne.com/mind-and-body/wabi-sabi/

36. Minhye Jung, "Kintsugi and the Art of Repair," *Kyō Journal* (blog), March 26, 2021, https://www.utne.com/mind-and-body/wabi-sabi/

37. Jung, "Kintsugi and the Art of Repair."

38. David A. Treleaven, *Trauma-Sensitive Mindfulness: Practices for Safe and Transformative Healing* (New York: W. W. Norton & Company, 2018).

39. See Rewire Therapy: https://www.rewiretherapy.net/ for daily somatic exercises to help re-regulate one's autonomic nervous system.

40. Hesychast has its roots in hesychasm, or the Greek συχασμός, hesychasmos, meaning "stillness, rest, quiet, silence." Hesychasm is an eremitic spirituality tradition of contemplative prayer that developed in Eastern Orthodox Christianity.

41. Ava Dasya Rasa, "After Silence," in *Earthsigns, An Anthology of Poems Commemorating the 2017 Haiku North America Conference.* Michael Dylan Welch and Scott Wiggerman, eds. (Sammamish: Press Here, 2017), 10.

42. H2617, *Strong's Hebrew Lexicon Number* accessed December 10, 2022. https://studybible.info/strongs/H2617.

43. Catholic Christian public and private examples of Cataphatic prayer include: the Rosary, praying with icons, the Stations of the Cross, Ignatian Spiritual Exercises, Chant, and Sacred liturgies.

44. Catholic Christian public and private examples of Apophatic prayer include: Centering Prayer, The Jesus Prayer (*Hesychasm* Eastern Christian Byzantine & Orthodox), Christian Zen meditation, and Mantra.

45. Ava Dasya Rasa, "I Sleep But My Heart Is Awake," (lecture, Unity Church, Santa Fe, NM, April 12, 2015).

46. Centering Prayer is not advised for persons suffering from unmanaged severe depression, dissociative identity disorder (DID), or psychosis.

47. See Appendix A: Guidelines for Centering Prayer.

48. "Lazarus Meaning," Abrahim Publications. https://www.abarim-publications.com/Meaning/Lazarus.html

49. "Zakar," BibleStudyTools.com https://www.biblestudytools.com/lexicons/hebrew/kjv/zakar.html

50. Rasa, "I Sleep But My Heart Is Awake."

51. Thomas Keating, *The Method of Centering Prayer, The Prayer of Consent* (Butler: Contemplative Outreach, LTD, 2016).

BIBLIOGRAPHY

Aeschylus. *Agamemnon*. Translated by Gilbert Murray. New York: Oxford University Press, 1920. The Guttenberg Project.

Anonymous. "Nineteen Old Poems." In *Chinese Poems*. Translated by Charles Budd. London: Oxford University Press, 1912. The Guttenberg Project.

Aristotle. *De Anima*. Translated by R. D. Hicks, MA. Cambridge: University Press, 1907. Internet Archive.

Aurelius, Marcus. *Meditations*. Translated by Méric Casaubon. London: J.M. Dent, 1905-1907. Internet Archive.

[Benedict, Saint, Abbot of Monte Cassino]. Prologue to *The Rule of St. Benedict*, 15. Edited by Timothy Fry, OSB. Collegeville: Liturgical Press, 1982.

Bible Study Tools. "Zakar." Accessed January 1, 2023. https://www.biblestudytools.com/lexicons/hebrew/kjv/zakar.html

Bourgeault, Cynthia. *Centering Prayer and Inner Awakening.* Read by Siiri Scott. Old Saybrook: Tantor Media, 2018. Audiobook, 6:50.

Bridgers, Lynn. *Contemporary Varieties of Religious Experience, James's Classic Study in Light of Resiliency, Temperament, and Trauma.* New York: Rowman & Littlefield Publishers, Inc., 2005.

Carroll, Lewis. *Alice's Adventures in Wonderland.* Philadelphia: Altemus, 1897. The Project Guttenberg.

Chryssavgis, John. *In the Heart of the Desert, The Spirituality of the Desert Fathers and Mothers.* Bloomington: World Wisdom, 2003.

Dana, Deb. *Befriending Your Nervous System.* Boulder: Sounds True, 2020. Audiobook, 8:24.

———. *The Polyvagal Theory in Therapy.* Read by Coleen Marlo. Old Saybrook: Tantor Media, 2019. Audiobook, 5:52.

De la Taille, Pere Maurice, SJ. *Contemplative Prayer.* London: Burns, Oates, & Washburn Ltd. 1926.

Dickinson, Emily. "A Timeline of Emily Dickinson's Life & Legacy." Emily Dickinson Museum. Accessed January 1, 2023. https://www.emilydickinsonmuseum.org/atimeline/#:~:text=1890%2C%20November%2012,Series%20(1896)%20of%20Poems.

———. "We Grow Accustomed to the Dark." The Adrian Brinkerhoff Poetry Foundation. Accessed December 29, 2022. https://www.brinkerhoffpoetry.org/poems/we-grow-accustomed-to-the-dark

Eckhart, Meister. *The Complete Mystical Works of Meister Eckhart.* Translated by Maurice O'C Walshe. Chestnut Ridge: Crossroad Publishing Co., 2009.

Estés Pinkola, Clarissa. *Women Who Run with the Wolves.* New York: Ballantine Books, 1992.

Fisher, Janina. *Healing the Fragmented Selves of Trauma Survivors.* Read by Emily Durante. Old Saybrook: Tantor Media, 2019, 14:41.

Frost, Robert Lee. "The Road Not Taken." In *Mountain Interval.* New York: Henry Holt and Company, 1916. Public Domain Poetry.

Gibran, Khalil. *The Prophet.* New York: Alfred A. Knopf, 1923. The Project Guttenberg.

Grand, David. *Brainspotting.* Boulder: Sounds True, 2013.

Griggs Lawrence, Robyn. "Wabi-Sabi: The Art of Imperfection." *Utne Reader.* Last modified October 27, 2007. https://www.utne.com/mind-and-body/wabi-sabi/

Hermann Lewis, Judith. *Trauma & Recovery.* New York: Basic Books, 1992.

Hughes, Langston. "The Negro Speaks of Rivers." In *The Crisis: A Record of the Darker Races*. New York: NAACP, 1921. Accessed on January 1, 2023. https://en.wikisource.org/wiki/The_Negro_Speaks_of_Rivers

Jung, Minhye. "Kintsugi and the Art of Repair," *Kyō Journal* (blog), Last modified March 26, 2021. https://www.utne.com/mind-and-body/wabi-sabi/

Levine, Peter A. *Waking the Tiger*. Berkeley: North Atlantic Books, 1997.

Lewis, Rhona. "Erikson's 8 Stages of Psychosocial Development, Explained for Parents. *Healthline*. Last modified April 28, 2020. https://www.healthline.com/health/parenting/erikson-stages

Kabir. *Songs of Kabir*. Translated by Rabindranath Tagore. New York, 1915. The Guttenberg Project.

Keating, Thomas. *The Human Condition, Contemplation and Transformation*. Mahwah: Paulist Press, 1999.

———.*The Method of Centering Prayer, The Prayer of Consent*. Butler: Contemplative Outreach, Ltd., 2016.

———.*Open Mind, Open Heart*. Warwick: Amity House, Inc. 1986.

Keating, Thomas, Pennington, M. Basil, and Clarke, Thomas E. *Finding Grace at the Center*. Still River: St. Bede's Publications, 1978.

Mechthild of Magdeburg. *Matelda and the Cloister or Hellfde*. Translated by Frances Bevan. London: James Nisbet & Co., 1896. The Guttenberg Project.

McGinn, Bernard, ed. *Mechthild of Magdeburg, The Flowing Light of the Godhead*. Mahwah: Paulist Press, 1998.

Merrill, Nan C. *Psalms for Praying, An Invitation to Wholeness*. New York: Continuum International Publishing Group, 2007.

McLeod, Frederick G. "Apophatic or Kataphatic Prayer?" *Spirituality Today*, Spring 1986, Vol. 38, 41-52. http://www.domcentral.org/library/spir2day/863815mcleod.html

Myss, Caroline and James Finely. *Transforming Trauma, Uncovering the Spiritual Dimension of Healing*. Boulder: Sounds True, 2010.

National Institute for the Clinical Application of Behavioral Medicine. "How To Help Your Clients Understand the Window of Tolerance." Accessed September 6, 2022. https://www.nicabm.com/trauma-how-to-help-your-clients-understand-their-window-of-tolerance/

Nietzsche, Fredrick Wilhelm. *Thus Spake Zarathustra*. Germany: Ernest Schmeitzner, 1883-1892. The Guttenberg Project.

Pennington, M. Basil. *Centering Prayer, Renewing an Ancient Christian Prayer Form*. New York: Doubleday, 1980.

Poet Unknown. "The Brevity of Life." In *Chinese Poems*. Translated by Charles Budd. London: Oxford University Press, 1912. The Project Guttenberg.

Porges, Stephen W. *The Polyvagal Theory: Neurophysiological Foundations of Emotions, Attachment, Communication, and Self-regulation (Norton Series on Interpersonal Neurobiology)*. New York: W. W. Norton & Company, 2011.

Rasa, Ava Dasya. "After Silence." In *Earthsigns, An Anthology of Poems Commemorating the 2017 Haiku North America Conference*, edited by Michael Dylan Welch and Scott Wiggerman. Sammamish: Press Here, 2017.

———."Bell Crickets." Santa Fe Haiku Group. Unpublished manuscript. October 1, 2018. Typescript.

———."I Sleep But My Heart Is Awake." Lecture. Unity Church, Santa Fe: April 12, 2015.

———."Silence." Unpublished manuscript. December 21, 2022. Typescript.

———."Wordless." Unpublished manuscript. December 21, 2022. Typescript.

Rogers, Carl R. "A Theory of Therapy, Personality, and Interpersonal Relationships: As Developed in the Client-Centered Framework." In *Psychology: A study of a science, Vol. 3, Formulations of the person and the social context,* edited by S. Koch, 184-256. New York: McGraw Hill, 1959.

Siegel, Daniel J. *The Developing Mind: towards a Neurobiology of Interpersonal Experience.* New York: Guilford Press, 1999.

Stein, Edith. "On the Problem of Empathy." In *The Collected Works of Edith Stein.* Translated by Waltraut Stein. Washington, DC: ICS Publications, 1989.

Stein, Gertrude. *Tender Buttons.* New York: Claire Marie Editions, 1914. The Guttenberg Project.

Swan, Laura. *The Forgotten Desert Mothers, Sayings, Lives, and Stories of Early Christian Women.* Mahwah: Paulist Press, 2001.

Symonds, John Addington. *The Sonnets of Michelangelo Buonarroti.* London: Smith, Elder & Co., 1904.

Teasdale, Sara. "The Rose." PoemHunter.com. Last Modified January 3, 2003. https://www.poemhunter.com/poem/the-rose/

Thoreau, Henry David. *Walden and the Duty of Civil Disobedience.* Boston: Ticknor and Fields, 1854. The Guttenberg Project.

Treleaven, David A. *Trauma-Sensitive Mindfulness: Practices for Safe & Transformational Healing.* New York: W. W. Norton & Company, 2018.

Van der Kolk, Bessel A. *The Body Keeps the Score, Brain, Mind, and Body in the Healing of Trauma.* Read by Sean Pratt. New York: Penguin Audio, 2021.

Warrack, Grace, ed. *Revelations of Divine Love.* London: Methuen and Company, 1901. The Guttenberg Project.

Weil, Simone. *Gravity and Grace.* New York: Routledge, 2007.

Welch-Kemp, Alice. *Of Six Mediaeval Women With a Note on Mediaeval Gardens.* London: Macmillan & Company Limited, 1913.

Whitman, Walt. "I Sing the Body Electric." In *Leaves of Grass.* Brooklyn: James and Andrew Rome Printing, 1855. Biblio. The Guttenberg Project.

———."Song of the Open Road." *In Leaves of Grass.* Brooklyn: James and Andrew Rome Printing, 1855. The Guttenberg Project.

Wiesenthal, Simon. "The Sunflower: On the Possibilities and Limits of Forgiveness." New York: Schocken, 1998.

Wilde, Oscar. *De Profundis.* London: Methuen & Co. Ltd, 1913. The Guttenberg Project.

FURTHER RECOMMENDED READING

Anonymous. *Cloud of Unknowing & Other Works*. New York, 1978.

Anonymous. *The Way of a Pilgrim and the Pilgrim Continues His Way*. New York 1985.

Br. Lawrence. *The Practice of the Presence of God: Critical Edition*. Washington, DC, 1994.

Bourgeault, Cynthia. *Centering Prayer and Inner Awakening*. Audible. Old Saybrook, 2018.

Chittister, Joan, OSB. *The Monastery of the Heart: An Invitation to a Meaningful Life*. New York, 2011.

Dana, Deb. *Polyvagal Exercises for Safety and Connection*. Audible. Old Saybrook, 2020.

De Chardin, Teilhard. *The Divine Milieu*. New York, 1968.

Deignan, Kathleen (Editor). *When the Trees Say Nothing: Thomas Merton's Writings on Nature*. Notre Dame, 2003.

De Waal, Esther. *Seeking God: The Way of St. Benedict*. Collegeville, 2001.

Eckhart, Meister. *The Essential Sermons, Commentaries, Treatises, and Defense*. Mahwah, 1981.

Finely, James. *The Contemplative Heart*. Notre Dame, 2000.

Grand, David. *Brainspotting*. Boulder, 2013.

Herman, Judith Lewis. *Trauma & Recovery: The Aftermath of Violence – from Domestic Abuse to Political Terror*. New York, 1992.

Keating, Thomas. *Finding Grace at the Center*. Still River, 1978.

———. *The Human Condition: Contemplation and Transformation*. Snowmass, 1999.

———. *Open Mind, Open Heart*. Warwick, 1986.

Levine, Peter A. *Waking the Tiger: Healing Trauma*. Berkeley, 1997

Maté, Gabor, and Daniel Maté, *The Myth of Normal: Trauma, Illness, and Healing in a Toxic Culture*. Read by Daniel Maté. Penguin Audio. New York, 2022.

Merrill, Nan C. *Psalms For Praying: An Invitation to Wholeness*. New York, 2007.

Merleau-Ponty, M. *Phenomenology of Perception*. London, 1981.

Merton, Thomas. *Seeds of Contemplation*. New York, 1953.

Nouwen, Henri J. *Out of Solitude: Three Meditations on the Christian Life.* Notre Dame: Ave Maria Press, 1974.

O' Donohue, John. *Anam Cara.* New York, 1997.

Ogden, Pat. *Trauma & The Body: A Sensorimotor Approach to Psychotherapy.* Audible. Old Saybrook, 2020.

Otto, Rudolf. *The Idea of the Holy.* Oxford, 1923.

Pennington, Basil M. *Centering Prayer, Renewing an Ancient Christian Prayer Form.* New York, 1980.

Perry, Bruce and Oprah Winfrey. *What Happened To You?: Conversations on Trauma, Resilience, and Healing.* New York, 2021.

Rohr, Richard. *Everything Belongs.* Chestnut Ridge, 2003.

———.*The Naked Now: To Learn to See as the Mystics See.* Audible. Holland, 2020.

Schwartz, Richard C. *No Bad Parts.* Boulder, 2021.

Schwartz, Arielle. *The Complex PTSD Workbook: A Mind-Body Approach to Regaining Emotional Control and Becoming Whole.* San Antonio, 2017.

Van der Kolk, Bessel A. *The Body Keeps the Score, Brain, Mind, and Body in the Healing of Trauma.* New York, 2015.

Waldron, Robert. *Poetry as Prayer: Thomas Merton.* Boston, 2000.

Whyte, David. *Consolations.* Langley: Many Rivers Press, 2020.

ACKNOWLEDGEMENTS

My deepest gratitude is extended first to three vitally important friends, all of whom have companioned me over the years of my own transfiguration journey, and who have recently passed from this life to their next. First, I remain forever grateful to my dear Mother, Betty Ann, for her enduring faith in me, empowering encouragement, and fervent prayers. I felt her championing me from heaven during the more intense periods of authoring this book. For Bob Lussier, OSB, spiritual director, for his hospitality, humor, and *hesed* in companioning me in our shared Benedictine spirituality; and, for M. Rose Theresa, OCD, for her unconditional love as my spiritual mother through all my "dangers, toils and snares." For my book publishing team, who applied their time and talent as readers, copyeditors, and graphic designers—especially, Joanne Vazquez, LCSW, who read the manuscript and offered her candid clinical insights, honest critique, and enthusiastic support; and Shrikesh Kumar for his kind patience and keen skills. For my extraordinary siblings and their incredible spouses, thank you for loving me as I walk my soul path. Lastly, to the Beloved, who called me by name, *I am yours*.

ABOUT THE AUTHOR

Ava Dasya Rasa, MSW, MA, LCSW-C is a transpersonal psychotherapist, specializing in trauma, grief, and contemplative spirituality & renewal. She is an author, poet, speaker, teacher, and spiritual director. Ava Dasya's clinical practice in neuro-based and somatic trauma therapies is informed by her decades of contemplative spiritual practice and extensive education into the transformation of grief and trauma. Ava Dasya is based in Albuquerque, New Mexico, where she is the Founder & CEO of Dragonfly Trauma Counseling Center. The Dragonfly symbolizes opportunity, change, transformation, adaptability, and new beginnings.

To learn more about Ava Dasya Rasa, please visit her author website at: www.avadasyarasa.com or Dragonfly Trauma Counseling Center at: www.dragonflytrauma.com

deo gratias

www.ingramcontent.com/pod-product-compliance
Lightning Source LLC
Chambersburg PA
CBHW031441160426
43195CB00010BB/815